Ransomed From Darkness
The New Age, Christian Faith and the Battle for Souls

He delivered us from the power of darkness
and transferred us to the kingdom of His beloved Son,
in whom we have redemption, the forgiveness of sins.
    — *Colossians 1, 13-14*

Ransomed From Darkness

The New Age, Christian Faith and the Battle for Souls

MOIRA NOONAN

NORTH BAY BOOKS
EL SOBRANTE, CALIFORNIA

Published by
North Bay Books
P. O. Box 21234
El Sobrante, California 94820
(510) 758-4276
www.northbaybooks.com

Comments and inquiries regarding this book may also be sent to
john@northbaybooks.com

Cover design by Elysium, San Francisco.
Distributed by Publishers Group West.
Manufactured in the United States of America.

Library of Congress Cataloging-in-Publication Data

[Available from the publisher]

Contents

Foreword

REV. JOHN HAMPSCH, C.M.F.

Amazement is an amazing emotion, inasmuch as it is found only in humans, as Aristotle noted. A dog or cat may have fear, joy, anger, guilt, or even surprise, but never amazement. Your pet cannot be amazed at the skill of a juggler, athlete, magician, tap dancer, singer or acrobat. Perhaps because it is exclusively human, amazement is an emotion that God often chooses to use for our spiritual persuasion, enticing us to love and praise him. The contemporaries of Jesus experienced amazement at his many healings, at his captivating speech, and even at his righteous indignation at the abuses of the money changers in the temple.

But to extend his evangelizing ministry to make disciples of all nations, Jesus often used others as his "instruments of amazement" — unskilled humans like Peter, Philip, Paul, Stephen, and countless other noble souls through the centuries — to excite changes of heart. Note, for example, how the astonishing behavioral change in the demonized maniac [Mark 5, 20] caused the citizens of the Decapolis to marvel at God's power. Through the ages, by giving their testimony to numerous marvels of divine power, wisdom and love, these human instruments of amazement have championed the glory of God. One such instrument of amazement used by God in our modern era is Moira Noonan, who has authored this instructive autobiography. Her life story is guaranteed to excite amazement in the reader, and, hopefully, to promote the praise of God for his goodness in seeking to lift his precious people from the quicksand of evil and to deflect the machinations of the Evil One.

If one were to propose a scriptural similitude of this book, it could well be Jesus' behest to the freshly exorcised Gerasene demoniac, who had sought companionship among the dead: "Return to your home, and declare how much God has done for you." [Luke 8, 39]

In this fascinating work Moira Noonan tells how, by Jesus' gentle heart tug, she was ransomed from the darkness of comradeship with the spiritually dead who thought they were alive. Having "returned to her home," the Church founded by Jesus, and by openly "declaring what God has done for her," she has chronicled the remarkable story of her life. Her encounters with subtle evils serve to alert the reader to the many beguiling dangers that lurk all around us: the "deceiving spirits" of the New Age movement that signal the end-times, spirits that Paul has warned about [I Tim. 4, I]. No one can read this book without rushing to Jesus, like a child encountering a pit of vipers who runs to the protective and loving arms of her father.

In that context, the amazement of the story becomes a mere prelude to a deeper emotion — and virtue: Love!

To the Sacred Heart of Jesus
and the Immaculate Heart of Mary,
in thanksgiving;
and in memory of my grandmother Katherine
and her saint, Therese, Little Flower of Jesus,
who never gave up on me;
and to my daughter Malia,
who somehow always knew
the Way, the Truth, the Life.

Preface

Ransomed From Darkness is a memoir and exposé of the New Age movement from the perspective of someone who was deeply involved in it for over twenty years. My purpose in writing it is twofold: first, to show to those who are participating in the movement its true origins and purposes, as I have learned from experience; second, to educate Christians who see New Age practices in their religious communities about the dangers these practices represent.

The book is divided into five parts. "Part One: My Life in the New Age," is an account of my personal journey into and out of the occult. It shows the true nature of the New Age movement by example, and the grace of God as He reaches out to rescue a soul in its snares.

After my conversion, I discovered the role I had to play in evangelizing those who had fallen prey to the same temptations I had. "Part Two: Stories of Conversion," describes four such cases. I might have included more, but these accounts show particularly well the intercession of Blessed Mother and the saints in the conversion process.

"Part Three: New Age Notebook," is a collection of short observations from talks I have given over the past decade that make points I feel are essential.

"Concerning *A Course in Miracles,*" Part Four, is a brief introduction to the history and ideas of a book that is nothing less than the bible of the New Age. It not only helps the reader to understand a demon-inspired philosophy that has taken root among many well-meaning Christians; it also emphasizes concepts that are fundamental, even for New Agers who have not been exposed to the Course directly. *Ransomed From Darkness* concludes with a look at how New Age ideas are entering the Church, and suggests steps that concerned Christians can take to reverse its continuing advance.

I have tried to be as accurate as possible, but some limitations could not be avoided. Out of consideration for the privacy of some, I have changed names and the specific details of certain events. Also, I cannot claim to have a flawless recollection of all my experiences and their exact chronology. Confusion, after all, is the Evil One's favorite tool, and parts of my history had to be retrieved through that cloud. Still, I am confident that any departures from perfect accuracy do not compromise the truthfulness of the narrative. Everything described here happened.

There are many people to thank, but I especially want to mention my daughter, Malia, who has been my best friend, comforter and teacher since she came into the world; Patrick Locke, who has kept audio and video records of nearly all my public presentations over the past decade; Rosemarie, a fellow convert and survivor of the New Age, who contributed to the section on the Course in Miracles; and Beverly Nelson C.M.C..

Above all, I give prayerful thanks to my Lord, Jesus Christ, Blessed Mother, and all the angels and saints, through whom I have been preserved and saved.

PRAYER TO ST. MICHAEL THE ARCHANGEL

St. Michael the Archangel, defend us in battle.
Be our protection against the wickedness and snares of
      the devil.
May God rebuke him we humbly pray.
And do thou, O prince of the heavenly host,
By the power of God, thrust into hell Satan
And all evil spirits who prowl about the world
Seeking the ruin of souls.
Amen.

Ransomed From Darkness

The New Age, Christian Faith and the Battle for Souls

Introduction
Principalities and Powers

"Put on the armor of God so that you may be able to stand firm against the tactics of the devil. For our battle is not with flesh and blood, but with the principalities, with the powers, with the world rulers of this present darkness, with the evil spirits in the heavens." So wrote St. Paul to the Christians at Ephesus, a city known throughout the ancient Mediterranean as a center of occult arts and pagan worship. [Ephesians 6, 11-12; Acts 19]

"Be sober and vigilant. Your opponent the devil is prowling around like a roaring lion looking for someone to devour." That's St. Peter, writing from Rome, shortly before his death, to Christians suffering persecution in the cities of Asia Minor. [1 Peter 5, 8]

Nearly two thousand years later I can tell you that these warnings of the apostles are still very real. They're not just old words in the Bible. Paul and Peter didn't talk about "world rulers of this present darkness" as a metaphor for abstract forces of evil, or to frighten the naive into embracing their faith. I have seen the confrontation they describe, and have been delivered from it.

"The whole of man's history has been the story of dour combat with the powers of evil stretching, so our Lord tells us, from the very dawn of history until the last day." That's the Catechism of the Catholic Church [CCC 408]. This battle, it explains, started at the very beginning of our presence on Earth, when the serpent promised our first ancestors that by eating from the Tree of the Knowledge of Good and Evil, their eyes would be opened and they would be like gods.

The language of the tempter will have a familiar ring to anyone who has dabbled in the New Age. So will the pride that inspired Adam and Eve to choose the forbidden fruit. "You are equal to God. You are the creator. You can realize your true divinity." These are the promises of the New Age. It offers beautiful fixes for life's difficulties, but many of its remedies are pathways by which demonic forces take hold in one's life. This is what happened to me. For more than twenty years I studied and practiced the teachings of dozens of esoteric schools, first in a search for relief from chronic pain, then as a passionate devotee of the New Age trinity: Me, Myself and I. In a few days I was delivered, and over the course of several years I was truly converted.

Writing an account of this experience has sometimes brought me to tears — tears of thanksgiving that we have such a holy and awesome God; that He could, as it says in Romans, chapter 8, make good of my past; that He could look upon my life in the occult and save me from it; that He could deliver me from such evil; that He could take up my soul that's been in such a battle and be my warrior and my savior. In gratitude, I break down and cry. And I thank God in the depth of my soul for my deliverance, and for being ransomed from this place of such darkness. Praise God.

Part One

Battle for a Soul

Chapter One
Erosion of Belief

Like many others who were to take up the banner of the New Age, I started out as a good Catholic schoolgirl. From kindergarten through second grade I went to convent schools in Detroit, then my family moved and I transferred to a public school, continuing my religious education at a local parish. There I completed CCD and received the sacraments.

In ninth grade I was sent to a Catholic boarding school far from home, Sacred Heart Convent in Philadelphia. It was an excellent school — so many times have I given thanks for those good sisters — but, at the end of my second year, there was a major fire. The school was destroyed. At the advice of a guidance counselor I was enrolled in another boarding school, a prestigious college preparatory academy in Massachusetts. This school was not Catholic. It was not religious at all. As a matter of fact, there was no encouragement to attend church, and thus I spent every Sunday on campus. In this way I missed years of sacraments and church and CCD, and all of the religious education one would normally get in a Catholic high school.

I was a curious sixteen-year-old at the time, readily open to influences, in a community without any Christian mentorship or role models. My spiritual curiosity was beginning to blossom, and because my roommate and best friend was Jewish, she and I sometimes went to synagogue together.

There was one teacher who became especially influential in our lives. She was one of our housemothers, as well as being our History teacher. This young woman was fascinated by India, and was, in fact, engaged to an Indian professor at Princeton University who would come to our school to take her out on dates. He would show up at our residence hall — a tall, dark, charming and brilliant man with a turban, and we got to be very friendly with him. Perhaps you can imagine at a boarding school, where we didn't have our parents around, how pleasant it was to have such interesting adults befriend us and take us to events on weekends. We went to Ravi Shankar concerts and learned about Indian music. He told us about meditation and gave us books about Indian philosophy. My housemother was so fascinated with Indian culture, she talked about it throughout the two years I spent at the school. In this way I learned a lot about Hinduism and other Eastern religions. By the time I graduated in 1970, I had decided that I would go to India someday, and that there I would find my guru and get enlightened.

Keep in mind: In the late 1960s much of the popular music, such as the Beatles and the Moody Blues, was written with intonations of Indian religion. The Beatles were introducing the world to Maharishi Mahesh Yogi, the founder of Transcendental Meditation, and they would go to India to stay at his ashram. At the same time dozens of Indian teachers were relocating their guru businesses to more lucrative American soil. Eastern religious influences were exploding onto the scene everywhere in America, and part of that thinking was that one needed to find a true spiritual guide, a living master, someone from whom you could learn directly, who could give you a mantra, or some secret technique, and take you to nirvana.

So this is how it started for me, this erosion of my Judeo-Christian belief system. It began with this seductively repackaged, Americanized Hinduism that was being sold to curious young Westerners. At the same time I couldn't help but be aware of the human potential movements that were also becoming popular. They, too talked about self-realization and self-enlightenment and seemed to confirm the ideas coming from the East. Did I fulfill my ambition to find a guru? No, I didn't. Not right away, at least. First I was headed for college.

Chapter Two
Enlightenment Postponed

After my graduation from boarding school I moved west and enrolled at a major state university. I still had in the back of my mind that I would go to India. That seed was firmly planted. On every campus billboard there were flyers posted — "Come to Meditate. Free Meditation Classes." — and I went to some of them. They were usually propaganda meetings to persuade people to follow a particular guru. The Rajneesh movement was very big in America at the time, and many of the meditation sessions were sponsored by his organization. Rajneesh ended up in a cult commune in the desert of eastern Oregon a few years later with ten or twenty Rolls Royces and a lot of legal problems. He has since been exiled from the United States and India and several other countries.

Drug use was also very big on campus, much more popular than religion. I was very turned off by that. I had a job after school, which I eventually had to quit because half the people I worked with were usually on drugs. All the elements of the counterculture movement began to compound for me — not only drugs, but also the anti-war conflicts, the questioning of our parents' values, the rejection of established institutions, the rebellion against the Church — to the point that I decided I needed to get away. After my sophomore year I left to study in Europe. I just didn't want to stay at school in America, and I kept thinking, "As soon as I'm done with college, I'll go to India to find my guru. If I'm in Europe, I'll be that much closer."

During my year abroad I traveled at every opportunity. When classes were finished, I went by train and boat to Greece, and then journeyed on to Turkey. At that point I thought I should just keep heading east. I could finish college some other time, and maybe I didn't really need college anyway. What I needed was enlightenment.

My grandmother back in Seattle saw things differently. She tried to track me down and somehow managed to reach me in Turkey by telephone. When she found out that I was planning to go to India, she knew what to do. She vowed to cut me off financially if I didn't come home right then and finish college. She suspected correctly that I had barely enough money left to get back to the US, let alone travel any further from home. So I returned to finish college and postponed my enlightenment until later.

I went to Seattle, moved in with my grandmother and resumed my work towards a degree at the University of Washington. I kept buying books about Eastern religion and went to a few meditation classes, but at the same time I would go to Mass occasionally with my grandmother — and always on holidays. At Mass, I didn't really think about or feel the true presence of Jesus in the Eucharist, and I really wasn't living my faith. I think I still believed in Blessed Mother and much of what I had been taught about Jesus. But I was convinced that what I really needed was a spiritual master living in the flesh, here and now.

Back and forth I went in my mind about these questions, until my fourth year of college arrived and I realized I needed to get focused on graduating. I went to Mass to please the family, not really participating in my faith, while my main goal was to work hard at my major, get good grades and prepare to get a job. By taking a bunch of extra credits I was able to graduate in June 1975 with a degree in Communications.

Chapter Three
A Brief Career

Coming out of school I got a great job doing public relations work for Francis Ford Coppola in San Francisco. He used to call me "the token blonde." Then I moved to Hawaii and went full speed into publishing. I dedicated myself completely to the role of the up-and-coming, career-oriented yuppie, making good money and working my way up the business ladder. Pursuing success in the world of magazines and newspapers leaves hardly any time for anything else, and I got completely out of spiritual search mode. I was no longer concerned with enlightenment at all. My only concern was making it big.

I got part of my wish. By the age of 28 I had bought and sold a newspaper, was the publisher of a tourist magazine, owned my own house and drove a nice car. I had investments to manage and bought real estate. It was the American dream: accumulating and consuming. Money and success and being what others said I needed to be were my gods.

And then one day, driving the company car, with half my office equipment stacked in the back seat and the trunk, I was involved in a major traffic accident. I was seriously injured, partially paralyzed and chronically in pain. Continuing my career was out of the question, and for the next two years my body barely functioned. For most of that time I was unable even to lift a coffee cup. As far as my doctors could tell, there was little or no hope of a complete recovery.

My relief began with a phone call from my sister, an attorney in California. "Moira, I've found out about this great pain clinic in the Midwest. They have a huge success rate helping patients with chronic pain. Insurance companies are sending patients there to get them off disability, so they can get well enough to get back to work. Do you think you could go there?"

For someone in constant pain and without hope, this was great news. I said, "Let's do it," and my sister got together with my insurance company to make the arrangements. I handed the magazine over to other people to run, rented out my house and flew from Honolulu to Wisconsin.

The clinic I entered there is now affiliated with the Menninger Clinic, but back then it was independent. Although it was fairly new, it was already being imitated by pain clinics across the country, at university hospitals and various other wellness centers. Almost all my expenses were covered by insurance, and to this day, when people ask me how my New Age experiences began, I tell them, "I owe it to my insurance company."

Chapter Four
New Thought Clinic

In the late 1970s, pain clinics were a relatively new phenomenon, and in many cases very experimental. Their main objective was to get patients off painkillers, off workers' compensation, and into forms of therapy that were less physically destructive and less expensive. The model used by some clinics, including the one I entered, was heavily influenced by the field of holistic health. One of the top neurosurgeons in the country had started it. After years of doing surgery on people's brains, he believed that he could help his patients control their pain more effectively by helping them to change their thought processes and belief systems.

During the five weeks I spent at the clinic, I followed a rigorous daily regimen, in which my mind was literally reprogrammed according to a system known as "New Thought." That's what they actually called it, "New Thought." This term comes from the book, *Science of Mind*, written by Ernest Holmes, which was first published in 1926. *Science of Mind* is the basic text for the Church of Religious Science and the Unity Churches, similar in spirit to the writings of Mary Baker Eddy, the founder of Christian Science.

To begin our treatment, the staff took away our pain medications and talked to us about the amazing powers of psychic healers in the Philippines and native shamans in South America. We watched videos of them at work. We then completed an exhaustive course in mind training called "autogenics." Basically this is hours and hours of self-hypnosis, reshaping the mind to conform to the reality we wished to create for ourselves. New Thought, we were told, was the answer to our problems. If we thought in a new way, we would free ourselves from guilt, and once were free from guilt, we would be free from pain. This was the kind of teaching that we got twenty-five years ago, and this is still going on today at university hospitals and pain clinics all over the country.

For ten hours each day we practiced pain-relieving techniques using subliminal audio tapes, biofeedback and other types of auto-suggestion — the same techniques, I was to learn later, that psychics use to learn out-of-body travel. We met almost daily with counselors and trainers and psychotherapists trained in New Thought methods. The messages that we were given were completely anti-Christian: "We're really not a body at all. There's no such thing as pain. It's just a thought and all we need to do is heal our thoughts." It was the kind of thinking that shapes the Course in Miracles, about which I'll have more to say later.

At no point did we hear about God as Creator. In fact, we were specifically told that, if we believed in a savior who would rescue us from our pain or protect us in times of stress and trauma, that was a waste of time. This kind of hope was like sitting on a rocking horse going nowhere. We had to do it ourselves. So there it was: the Holy Trinity of Me, Myself and I, creeping in through the back door.

They rejected the idea that there could be any type of

virtue in suffering, any value in bodily pain or illness. Pain was not of God, it was against God, All of my former belief systems, all of my attitudes toward the body, toward life in general, toward God, toward healing, were erased. As this program eliminated my need for pain medications, it also washed away my understanding of the world, eroding the Judeo-Christian beliefs I had received as a child and replacing them with new ones, free of suffering and free of God.

The fact is, I was attracted to all this. After all, even though I had stopped taking pain pills, my health had improved dramatically. My body was functioning well for the first time in years. The system worked. I even had some quite powerful out-of-body sensations, which excited me, and so I became deeply interested in the beliefs and philosophies of the clinic. I asked a lot of questions. The therapists and doctors and staff members, I learned, all shared the same spiritual ideas. You are beyond matter. You are not a body. You create your own reality. This all fit in just fine with what I had been learning since high school about reincarnation and meditation.

As the end of the fifth week approached and I began to anticipate my return to active life, I felt the need to ask my teachers about going to church. They said I would need spiritual support, but the Catholic Church was definitely not the place to look for it. In order to stay free of pain I needed to stay in the New Thought frame of mind, and only certain churches offered this: Unity Churches, the Christian Scientists, Dianetics — these kinds of groups. They also gave me more autogenic tapes and meditations and other self-hypnosis tools. By taking advantage of these resources, they promised me, I was sure to remain pain-free.

So I want to warn you: Watch out where your body ends up. If you find yourself in the wrong place in the wrong hands, you can open yourself to influences that are basically demonic.

People have said to me, "My chiropractor always dangles a crystal on a string over my back before working on me. What's that all about?"

I ask them, "How did you find this chiropractor?"

"I read about him in the church bulletin."

"Well, let me tell you, this is a crystal pendulum and he's using it to check the condition of your energetic body. He's practicing psychic healing arts when you thought you were just going to get your spine adjusted. Find a new chiropractor — and talk to your church about the bulletin!"

I like to warn Christians about this kind of thing; it happens all the time. The danger is that one thing leads to another. Increasingly we believe that we can do everything ourselves. We are the doers, and there are benign spiritual forces that can help us. With their assistance we can influence God's plan. It is through this kind of thinking that demon spirits inflate the ego, sometimes to the point that we believe that we are creator gods, that we can manifest, that we can do it ourselves. This kind of brainwashing, replacing my Judeo-Christian beliefs with New Thought, was the sprouting of the New Age seed planted in me back in boarding school.

Chapter Five

The Gospel of Religious Science

When I returned to Hawaii I was completely off medication and without pain. But in order for this to continue, I needed to keep hypnotizing myself on a regular basis. I took the clinic's advice to heart and went out right away in search of spiritual support. I joined a Unity Church, and was very interested in everything they were doing. Once again I was in search mode. New Thought religion was certainly a lot easier than going all the way to India and looking for a guru, and I decided to become a Unity church minister. The gospel I now embraced goes back to Mary Baker Eddy, the founder of the Christian Science Church. It claims that we are all divine; we are, each of us, our own god and co-creator with other divine forces. The Jesus I accepted was a Gnostic Jesus, whose spiritual identity was "infallible," but whose incarnation "was not Christ."

This idea was pretty mainstream compared to some of the ideas I had been exposed to. But it represented a breaking of the First Commandment, "You shall have no other gods besides Me." This is the foundation of our faith, and if it's broken, all the others follow. I broke the First Commandment, and eventually this would lead me into all the forms of idolatry listed in the book of Deuteronomy [18, 9-12]: fortune telling, soothsaying, divination, casting of spells and contacting the dead. I was to become involved in pretty much

every single one of these practices, some of them profession-
ally.

My plans to become a Unity Church minister never quite
materialized. Before I got very far in my training I decided to
get married. A little later a child was on the way, bringing new
priorities. Thank you, Lord. My husband and I sat down and
decided to leave Hawaii in order to raise our daughter on the
mainland. There were many reasons, but especially, I think,
because in those years drugs — marijuana and that type of
thing — were so prevalent in Hawaii, even in grade schools. I
just thought raising a child would be better in California.

After our move, the closest New Thought church was a
Church of Religious Science, a twentieth-century offshoot
of the Unity churches, also based on the ideas of Ernest
Holmes. I decided to join. Now something kind of interesting happened while I was pregnant with my daughter, something that I am certain played a role in my eventual redemption.

I took a holiday trip to Europe with my mother. One
morning while we were in Paris, my mother said, "Come to
Mass with me." So we went to the Basilica of Sacré Coeur,
this glorious church at the top of Montmartre, dedicated to
the Sacred Heart of Jesus Christ. There we found the most
beautiful statue of Our Lady, and there were candles in front
of it. Somehow — it must have been the Holy Spirit — I was
compelled to light a candle there for my unborn child. I didn't
know at that point how to consecrate her to Our Lady, but
something inside moved me. My mother wasn't even with me

when I did this; she was kneeling in the pews. I just went over and lit a candle, and said silently, "Blessed Mother, this is your child. I give this child to you."

So, again, thank you, Sacred Heart nuns. Something you told me stayed in my mind. Something told me to go light the candle and give this child to Blessed Mother and I did. It has definitely saved her from a lot. When my child was born, we named her Malia, which is "Mary" in Hawaiian.

As Malia grew out of infancy, the possibility of becoming a minister again attracted me. I liked the system of Religious Science, and they used the same book, *Science of Mind,* that the Unity churches used. So I basically picked up my New Thought education where I had left off a few years earlier and entered ministry training. The program takes four years.

New Thought, I now know, is really a form of brainwashing that leads to the abandonment of all the Commandments and replaces them with the New Age Holy Trinity I have already mentioned: Me, Myself and I. I now call New Thought churches "Churches of Manifestation." They are all about manifesting one's wishes. Their teachings have nothing to do with such Christian ideals as surrendering to the will of God, or receiving the gifts of the Holy Spirit. They are about the belief that I can do it, that as I activate my "I am" presence, I will be the manifestor. Many of their techniques have their roots in the nineteenth-century psychology of Franz Mesmer, who is best known as a developer of the science of hypnosis.

We learned to pride ourselves on how much we could manifest. For example, we'd write up these little cards. "I really need to," let's say, "have $5,000 by such and such a date." And then we would try to manifest that wish through prayer and meditation. We learned how to be prayer practitioners and give prayer treatments to others for physical and psychological healing. I was introduced to the psychic arts of clairvoyance and clairaudience. It was really a lighter presentation of the kinds of serious occult practices I was to learn later.

Be aware that these practices are for real; they're not tricks. They are related to what's called "spiritualism," which the Bible warns us against. In Deuteronomy and elsewhere, God makes it very clear: Stay away from mediumship, sorcery and fortune telling of all kinds. Jeremiah warned the people not to look for signs of the future in the stars. The Bible makes it clear, over and over: Don't go to these kinds of places. That was a message I had never received. [*See* Deuteronomy 18, 9-14; Leviticus 20, 27; Acts 16, 16-18; CCC 2116]

By this time my grandmother and the rest of my family were concerned that I was going off the deep end. They would send me Christian books on spiritual warfare and the lure of the occult. They were trying to get me out of it, but I was headed in the other direction. You see, the more you work with the sense of "I am," the more your ego is built up. And when you start manifesting, as your teachers promise you will, the power of creating seduces you.

I remember well how big a shock it was for me, after I had left the movement and returned to the Church, when some Catholic women told me I was "a creature of the Creator." I had just spent twenty years understanding that I was a creator. I could manifest anything because I was a god. And now these women were telling me I'm a creature of the Creator. I thought they were absolutely crazy. That's how brainwashed I was. That's how off the wall it gets. You really believe you can do anything and everything. Your dependency on the self is very, very powerful.

Once my ministry training was finished, I began to serve as a leader at a Religious Science church north of San Diego. My daughter had attended preschool at New Age churches and was now a student in the Religious Science Sunday school. One day — I think she was six years old — she came to me and said, "Mom this isn't right. I don't like what they're teaching me."

I thought, "What do I do? This is where I've got to go every Sunday. How can I deal with this? Maybe I could leave her at someone's house every Sunday morning." I didn't know what to do. It didn't occur to me to send her to a Catholic church. I thought they would never accept her anyway, since her mother had drifted so far off. Surely they wouldn't accept her while her mother believed as I did. I just didn't know what to do, so I prayed about it. In the Church of Religious Science I had been trained to pray in a manifesting way, but for some reason my prayer came out different. "God, if you do not want Malia to go to this church, where would you like her to go?"

The answer came soon. A few weeks later, Malia and I

were at the neighborhood swimming complex when a woman I barely knew walked up to me and said, "Do you have your child in Sunday school?."

I responded without a pause, "How nice of you to offer!"

I knew that the woman was interrogating me, but I also understood it as an offer, and I accepted. This woman, it turns out, felt it was part of her mission to bring children to Sunday school. She went to a Lutheran Church. I didn't know anything about Lutherans, but I knew it was Christian so I figured, "That must be where she's meant to go."

"Good," she said. "I'll pick your child up every Sunday morning. I want her completely dressed and ready to go by 8:30, and she'll go to church with us."

I thought, "Thank you, God. This must be right," and for the next five years my daughter went with the neighbors to the Lutheran Church.

When Malia announced that she was about to have her first Communion, I was still working at the Church of Religious Science in Del Mar. I decided to read the Sunday School books she was using to prepare because I had this feeling that something was missing. Then I took Malia aside and said, "I don't want to offend the neighbors, but I know that when I had first Communion in the Catholic Church, what we were taught was different than what Lutherans are taught. Do you think you would be willing to go to first Communion at a Catholic Church as well?"

I had just read something about Our Lady visiting Medjugorje, and I felt in some inexplicable way that it was important for Malia to have her Catholic sacraments. I called up St. John the Evangelist Catholic Church in Encinitas and spoke to the secretary there, told her I was a New Ager, that I was in ministry with the Church of Religious Science, but that I wanted my daughter to get first Communion in the Catholic Church. I also made it clear that I was not going to church there and I had no intention of doing so.

Cindy, the secretary, was fantastic. She took my daughter under her wing. She brought her to Monday night CCD so it wouldn't interfere with the neighbors and their Sunday program. So while Malia went to class and services at the Lutheran church on Sunday and CCD at the Catholic church on Monday, I continued my work as a New Age minister. My daughter is grown up now, and Catholic, and full of gratitude for our neighbors. They protected her soul from any further New Age influences, and from the psychic warfare I was to get involved in later.

Chapter Six
Psychic Doorway

When I think about my years in the New Age movement, I think of opening doors. On the one hand, my role in Religious Science ministry opened doors for me into dozens of esoteric practices, many of which I was able to explore in depth. On the other hand, these open doors were pathways by which demonic spirits entered my life.

Much of my early ministry education, for example, was focused on developing psychic abilities. I started on this path by exploring seemingly harmless aspects of extra sensory perception — mind reading, fortune telling, and so forth. The more I learned, the more curious I became about what the psychic world had to offer. I joined a teaching program in the "I Am" teachings, which trained us to use the "Third Eye." Third Eye refers to the eye of the mind that sees into the spirit world. The round mark that traditional Hindu women display between and just above their eyes is a symbol of this.

By working with Third Eye techniques I became an accomplished clairvoyant. A clairvoyant is one who sees into the past, present and future. This is different than a psychic who is clairaudient, one who gets information by hearing, or a clairsentient, one who does so by feeling. I received information by seeing, which means I saw movies playing in my mind. When someone came to me for psychic counseling, I could see events of their life flashing before me and know many things about them — personal things.

Psychic abilities are not the same as the gifts of prophecy and knowledge from the Holy Spirit that Paul talks about in I Corinthians, chapter 12. People who receive the gifts of the Holy Spirit are anointed through divine action by the divine will. People cannot create or develop such gifts on their own, as if they were the doer. Also, psychic abilities invite spiritual invasions that create confusion and anxiety. The gifts of the Holy Spirit bring peace.

As I became more psychically proficient, I actually began to see angels and demons. I saw so many things, most of which I didn't want to see. Demons, after all, don't approach one gently, asking, "Do you have time for me now?" Once the door is open they bombard you. I eventually found it hard to sleep because my mind was always rushing, without interruption, like Grand Central Station. Shutting off the movie was out of my control. Ask almost anyone who has been a psychic, especially a clairvoyant. They will tell you the same thing: They have no peace. Yes, there is a spiritual battle for souls going on and anyone involved in the occult is aware of it.

In the end I was in desperate need of help. Psychics would say I needed to "get cleared." The only solution I could think of at the time was to go to other psychics but, of course, that didn't work. So, let me tell you, if you encounter anyone who has reached this level of psychic awareness, please evangelize them. Ask them, "Would you like to stop seeing these things? Would you like to be saved from that world?" Because at that level of adeptness, they have sold a part of their soul, and they know it. They have no peace. They see into demon worlds and they don't like it — I didn't like it. Such people are ripe to be evangelized. Don't feel shy. Talk to them. Tell them Jesus is the Prince of Peace.

Now that I'm back in the Catholic faith, I know what it was that I was seeking. I have heard from other former psychics who were raised Catholic and have come back to their faith. They, too, were actually looking for the gifts and the fruits of the Holy Spirit. They were just looking in the wrong places. Now they can sleep at night. Praise God.

Chapter Seven
Healing Arts

My experience at the pain clinic inspired me to delve deeply into the field of hypnotherapy. I became a certified Ericksonian hypnotherapist with a special interest in past-life regression. Past-life regression is a technique by which a person is guided back in time in order to observe experiences in previous lives. The New Age movement promotes such therapies because, according to its teachings, people fail to manifest things in their present lives — money, love, health — because of the way they think. Their thinking is shaped, in part, by things that happened in past lives, which block their progress in the present. Past-life regression therapies, so they say, clear those blocks so that the abundant flow of god-energy, which is ever-present, will come back into them and through them. Once this force is recaptured, a person can use it to create his own reality. Past-life regression enables one to work with the laws of the universe and get beyond time and space, which, after all, is just an illusion anyway.

Regression therapies are, of course, only meaningful if one believes in reincarnation, a belief that is fundamental to New Age thinking. According to the doctrine of reincarnation we have many lifetimes in which to achieve enlightenment, or self-realization. Indeed, in any system where a person functions as his own savior, more than one lifetime would certainly be required!

I know now that the past-life experiences I once induced were either imaginary, or were drawn from experiences earlier in a client's present life. Some may have involved the work of dark forces, but most likely they didn't. Reincarnation, as we know from Hebrews 9, 27, was certainly not a factor.

Not all forms of hypnotherapy, however, are dangerous, and in fact, in many cases it can change destructive behavior patterns. What makes it risky, however, is that a person under hypnosis has surrendered his will and is utterly open to suggestion. So you must know the background and belief system and training of anyone who provides you with hypnosis therapies. It all has to do with the will. Whenever you are hypnotized you surrender your will, and are extremely vulnerable to any influences that the therapist brings to her work. For me personally, it is a can of worms that I prefer to stay away from.

Another psychic healing system I was involved in is Reiki. Reiki is a method of healing through the transmission and activation of a person's spiritual energy. This therapy looks somewhat like the Christian laying on of hands, but this is deceptive. The symbolism of Reiki is deeply influenced by Buddhist traditions, and invisible spirit guides — demon spirits — are specifically invoked by name to confer their healing powers. Reiki is also highly esoteric, and a personal apprenticeship with a Master Healer, a designation I eventually earned, is required. To set down its laws in writing is forbidden.

Twenty-five years ago Reiki was a fairly exotic practice, but in the years since it has found its way into some surprising places. Some of the most expensive and reputable spas in places like Palm Springs offer Reiki treatments. I have seen brochures that describe it as an Oriental blend of Swedish and Shiatsu massage, but that's far from the truth. I'm also aware of several places where Catholic nuns have learned Reiki and offer it as an alternative to conventional healing therapies. But believe me, the spirit guides of Reiki are not reconcilable with the Holy Spirit. If a well-meaning Christian were to replace Reiki symbols with Christian symbols and call upon the name of Jesus it would no longer be Reiki. It would be charismatic healing, which is a completely different practice.

Among the most widely recognized teachers of New Age healing using spirit guides is Barbara Brennan, author of *Hands of Light* and the founder of The Barbara Brennan School of Healing, now located in Boca Raton, Florida. A former research scientist at NASA, Brennan does not call her system "Reiki," but the content of "Brennan Healing Science" is similar. I perfected my skills at her Institute.

As Brennan herself admits, her ideas are drawn from direct communication with a spirit guide named Heyoan. Her channelings from this entity are regularly published word for word by her institute and offered to the world as expressions of divine wisdom. This is what I mean when I talk about the role of demons in the practice of Reiki, or any other psychic healing art that uses spirit guides.

As a practitioner I had a spirit guide of my own. Years later, when I recited to the last detail my experiences in the occult during confession, the priest who heard me was a man with a special gift for working with returning New Agers. When I mentioned Reiki, Father Philip Pavich knew the forces I was talking about. He actually knew the names of Heyoan and other spirits that were attached to Reiki. He knew Heyoan and his crew were adversaries of the Holy Spirit, and he was able to deliver me from them.

Chapter Eight
Teachings of the Inner Christ

Another place I studied was called Teachings of the Inner Christ, which at the time was based in Lemon Grove, near San Diego. This group teaches that the historical Jesus was an "ascended master," an enlightened being and member of a group of heavenly immortals called the "Great White Brotherhood." This omniscient council helps earthbound human beings to attain higher levels of consciousness and the psychic powers that go with them. In this cosmology "Christ" actually means "Christ Consciousness," a state of awareness that every person has the potential to achieve if they observe the laws of self-realization that the White Brotherhood has set in motion.

Inner Christ proponents don't actually consider themselves New Agers. They are more in line with that older tradition known as spiritualism. For example, they do seances where they call forth spirits of the dead and ask them about life in the next world. We were actually trained to do this, and I got be very good at it, because as a clairvoyant I had already developed my capacity to see spirits. Even though I was not trained as a clairaudient, I could hear them as well. My instructor, Dr. Ann Makeever, a co-founder of Teachings of the Inner Christ, was quite adept and had almost every occult skill. She claimed the ability to see, hear, feel and smell the presence of spirits.

People often came to our seances in order to contact

loved ones who had passed away. That is not what they saw. The truth is they called upon demons without knowing it. The demons would play whatever roles they were asked to — relatives, spirit guides, familiar people. The Catholic Church calls this necromancy, and you can look it up in the Catechism [2116] as well as in the book of Deuteronomy [18, 11]. These texts specifically forbid Christians to practice necromancy.

At the time I had no idea that the work of Teachings of the Inner Christ was demonic. Their courses covered a number of enlightenment-related subjects that made perfect sense once the First Commandment was set aside. Jesus himself, we were taught, along with another ascended master out of India, Babaji, brought messages of peace and inner harmony to the world through Dr. Makeever and her followers. I was deceived by this, and so were many others.

In our weekly programs at the Teachings of the Inner Christ Center, Hollywood types often came down to participate. I remember the cast and crew of the television series *The Love Boat* attending some of our seances. We would place our fingers on the edge of a table — there would be people all around it — and then we would call upon the ascended masters, who would begin to lift and rock the table. We called it "table-tipping." We would do the same thing with chairs and other furnishings. These tricks seemed to validate the metaphysical teachings of the group, which are entirely incompatible with the teachings of the Church.

Researchers from NASA even came to photograph us.

They later published a photograph of a table as it was being lifted. In the picture, the table legs appear as four bright beams of light, supposedly energy beams.

On a regular basis Dr. Makeever would organize large events at the Masonic Temple in San Diego. We would publicize these gatherings by word of mouth in the New Age Community — the Science of Mind Churches and so forth. People would come from all over Southern California, including, again, a number of Hollywood celebrities. Seances and table tipping sessions with more than 500 people in attendance would go on for hours. Everyone in the temple was thinking. "Wow! Here we have a genuine connection to the spiritual world." But the connection was to the allies of Lucifer, the ultimate angel of darkness, who loves to pose as an angel of light.

Chapter Nine
Visions of Masters

It would have been surprising if my New Age life did not include initiation rites with an Indian guru. After all, part of my original plan was to travel to India in search of a teacher, and even without this journey, guides to enlightenment from the East were hard to avoid in the 1980s, especially in Southern California. They still are today.

I took initiation with several gurus. During initiation a spiritual master usually gives his student a mantra, often a set of words or letters from the Sanskrit language, which the student is told to repeat in meditation in order to reach higher states of consciousness. Then by look or touch the teacher awakens energy in the student that, with time and discipline, will fuel the journey to self-realization. Comparisons have been made with the Christian tradition of baptism, particularly in the case of Jesus himself and John the Baptist. Again the similarities are deceiving. For one thing, the god behind a guru's initiation is always the guru himself.

I was initiated by a well-known figure named Sant Thakar Singh, a Sikh teacher from the Himalaya then living in the United States. In the guru business, lineage is important, and Thakar Singh's is fairly ancient, most recently passing through two well-known Indian teachers, Kirpal Singh and the master who preceded him, Sawan Singh. Initiates into such lineages report many different experiences, some including powerful visions. In my own case, at Thakar Singh's touch his own masters, Kirpal Singh and Sawan Singh, both long dead, appeared to me. I saw them in the room with us watching the event with approval. I interpreted this a sign of acceptance.

That night, after I had returned home and gone to bed, I heard a knock at my front door. The sound woke me from a light sleep, and I lay their thinking, "I wonder who could be knocking at this hour?" It seemed very strange.

I got out of bed, put on my robe and went down the stairs. The stairs face the front door, and at that moment the door gently opened and Thakar Singh, who had given me initiation only a few hours before, and Sawan Singh, smiling benevolently in his long white beard, entered my house.

These two phantom forms came up the stairs and followed me back into my bedroom suite, and there presented me with a vision of light and sound. As I lay on the bed in the darkened room, with the two turbaned figures standing nearby, I was drowned in the most beautiful celestial music anyone could ever imagine, and shown bright, colorful visions of grandeur and beauty. Without words my gurus were saying to me, "Here is a gift for you, most welcome disciple."

I associate this event with an experience I had later at the headquarters of Elizabeth Clare Prophet's church, Summit Lighthouse, which was then based in Malibu. Prophet is another teacher who channels messages from the Great White Brotherhood. I attended a number of her programs before her organization moved to Montana, where she now lives. On this particular day I happened to be en route to Mt. Shasta, a snow-covered, volcanic peak in Northern California, regarded by many as the home of another ascended master, St. Germaine. I decided to stop in Malibu to see if I could get more information about my destination.

This was my first visit to Summit Lighthouse, and at that point all these masters and brotherhoods were still pretty new to me. As I walked through the empty church, I found myself strongly affected by an icon hanging on the wall, a portrait of El Morya, the particular ascended master with whom Elizabeth Clare Prophet is most closely identified. El Morya is said to be based in Darjeeling, India, and to have been born in human form as Abraham, Melchior, King Arthur, Thomas Becket, Thomas More, and a few other reputable historic figures.

As I stood gazing upon his picture, the form of El Morya literally jumped out of the frame and landed a few feet in front of me. I didn't feel any fear. I spontaneously fell to my knees in a posture of submission. At that moment I felt he must be my savior. I was consumed by an awareness of his power over me, and as a result, vowed to follow him. In the months afterward I read everything about him that I could get my hands on, building for him a place in my gradually expanding pantheon.

Chapter Ten
Spirits of the Lake

One common feature of the New Age is the spiritual retreat. Retreats are one of the most popular methods by which New Age teachers reach students directly. Some groups have their own centers to which people come to study with a particular authority. More often, a retreat center will host teachers from many different schools, in a schedule that includes weekend and week-long sessions throughout the year. Popular retreat centers include the Omega Institute in New York, Questhaven in Southern California, Esalen in Big Sur and Hollyhock in Canada. Communities such as Sedona, Arizona, have a thriving retreat industry.

I spent part of several summers in residence at a well-known retreat center in the rural Northeast. I would go there for a month or six weeks, and register in every workshop and seminar they had to offer. This center was one of the most prestigious in the country and, in a way, served as an intensive annual graduate program in New Age sciences. Shamanism, yoga, bodywork and meditation were part of the annual fare.

At this institute there is a beautiful little lake, and that lake has a history to it. The whole property has a history to it, in fact. It gets very hot there in the summer and many retreat participants, at some point, head for the lake to swim. On one especially hot day I went down to the lake with the rest of the crowd. I sat alone for a few minutes on the sandy beach to collect my thoughts, and at once had the sensation that something was wrong. I felt that there was something very strange and forbidding about this lake, even though it was a calm, sunny day and everyone was obviously having fun. So many people were enjoying themselves in the cool water and the mountain air, playing outdoors after a morning of workshops, that I decided my feelings must be mistaken.

The lake had a platform anchored out in deep water that people would swim to, sun bathe on and dive from. I put my suit on, jumped in the water and swam out to it. By the time I reached the platform the dark emotion I felt had completely overwhelmed me. I lifted myself out of the water and, sitting there in the middle of the lake, surrounded by contented sun bathers, I began to cry uncontrollably. I couldn't stop, I knew something was very wrong, and I kept crying and crying, and I thought, "How am I going to get back to the shore?" It was as if I had been literally swimming through spirits. It was just eerie and it was sickening. It felt like I was swimming through blood, it was just so thick. I couldn't stand it.

After I swam back to shore I showered, dressed and went to dinner. In the café I went right up to the director of the center, a well-known alternative medicine teacher and author, and asked him, "Dr., what do you know about the history of this land and that lake. Did something happen here?"

He turned and looked straight at me. I don't think we had ever talked before. He said, "What do *you* know?"

"I went swimming this afternoon out to the dock. When I was in the water I just started crying. I couldn't stop. I felt I was swimming through blood. I could feel the presence of spirits — a lot of them."

"What is your name?"

When I told him, he paused for a moment and then answered, "Well, Moira, there is something about that lake, and I'll tell you what it is. This area was colonized by white settlers. Originally the land was a summer home for native people, who used to camp along the shores. This was their source of fish and water and medicine. They lived along the shore where we are sitting right now. When the white settlers came over the hills and wanted to take the land, they didn't ask for permission. They just rushed in. There was a bloody massacre and they killed every Indian — man, woman and child, all of them. They didn't bother to bury the corpses. They threw their bodies into the lake."

Now this doctor, a physician in charge of a major New Age center, supposedly an authority in spiritual matters, acted as though that was the end of it. "That's what happened here. That's the way it is." As if there were nothing more to be done.

No one has ever performed a deliverance service there. In the New Age, they don't understand deliverance. The most they will do is put on a show with crystals and chants, but what is needed is a healing Mass for the land. There are priests who are experienced in this.

Chapter Eleven
First Sign Along the Path

I have no doubt that it was Blessed Mother who guided me out of the anxiety, confusion and darkness of the New Age. She set along my path a series of small signs. I followed them without knowing where I was being led, or even that I was being led at all. The first sign that I recall now appeared during morning coffee break at a New Age workshop in Hawaii.

More than a decade had passed since my move to California. I was practicing past-life regression with my hypnotherapy clients. I was also interested in an emerging new field called Neuro-Linguistic Programming. NLP is a form of behavior modification that has been popularized by, among others, Anthony Robbins. You have probably heard of him. Robbins is one of the most widely sought-after motivational speakers in America. You will see him on cable TV infomercials, featured in bookstores, and also in a few motion pictures. His credibility extends to some of the country's largest corporations — even to the White House. Robbins' Neuro-Linguistic Programming is, in fact, extremely advanced hypnotherapy: change your state, change your thoughts, change your mind, change your life, get what you want. This is the basic thinking of his movement.

A doctor in Maui who was both an expert in Ericksonian hypnotherapy and a consultant with the Anthony Robbins group was offering an intensive course in past-life regression therapy, incorporating Ericksonian techniques using NLP. I signed up for the program and went back to Hawaii for a short period, completely unaware of the turn my path was about to take.

One morning, as I sat passing the time between sessions, I picked up a copy of *New Age Journal*, which was lying nearby on a side table. At the time *New Age Journal* was the largest circulation New Age magazine in America. There I found an article by one of the more visible personalities of the movement, Sondra Ray. Ray described an experience she had had while traveling to India to meet her guru, Babaji. Her guru, she wrote, is what's called an "immortalist." At different times in the history of the world he is reborn. No human procreation is involved; he simply manifests in his cave in India. This type of story always fascinated us: an American woman who could go and actually meet up with some guy in a cave in India, who was immortal, who had just come back into a human body for the twentieth time, who had no parents, the Himalayan mountains looming up all around.

Ray reported that as she waited in London's Heathrow Airport for a connecting flight to New Delhi, she happened to read a story about Mother Mary appearing at Medjugorje, in Yugoslavia. Immediately she felt an overwhelming call to go see what this was all about. She hastily changed her itinerary and arranged to stop in Yugoslavia on her way to India.

This was the first time I gave serious thought to the meaning of Our Lady appearing to people in modern times.

It was 1991. I was captivated by the idea that this very progressive woman, who was not raised Catholic, not even Christian, would fly and drive and taxi all the way to Yugoslavia, to
Medjugorje, to St. James Church. According to the article,
she was standing outside the church when a priest invited her
into the upper room to witness the young visionaries. Ray
gave a full description of what she saw there. She did not see
Our Lady. She said that only the children could see. But she
felt deeply Our Lady's presence. Ray didn't experience a conversion, but her article was riveting.

The unfortunate thing about the article, however, was
Ray's account of what happened after her visit to Medjugorje.
She traveled on to India and New Zealand and Australia and
back to America. Once she was settled at home she concluded
that Our Lady must be a goddess. "Mother Mary," she wrote,
"is the goddess from Heaven come down to meet the Earth
goddess."

As I read this, somehow, I knew it wasn't right. The article was tremendously powerful. It hit me right in the heart,
but I knew, even though I was so indoctrinated in New
Thought, that Blessed Mother was not a goddess. Thank you
again, Sacred Heart nuns. Some truth stuck. Praise God for
you.

Sondra Ray later went on to write books about the goddess phenomenon and organized a series of related workshops, which have been held all over the country. Out of these
events has grown an enormous false Mary movement. *The Wall
Street Journal* covered a Marian conference in Montana, for ex-

ample, hosted by Elizabeth Clare Prophet's Summit Lighthouse, where they claim to have channeled Mother Mary. More than 5,000 people attended. Goddess workshops are even offered at Dominican and Benedictine retreat houses. Satan, you see, mimics and mocks absolutely everything in the Catholic faith.

So as I read Sondra Ray's words I knew that Our Lady was not a goddess. She was not like Artemis, the pagan patroness of Ephesus worshiped in the time of Paul. Deep down I knew that she was the mother of Jesus, a real, live Jewish woman who lived two thousand years ago, who walked this same earth. Moved and confused at the same time, I had to leave the workshop. I went to the seashore for a long solitary walk, and there I was inspired to form a sincere prayer in my heart. "God, if the mother of Jesus is appearing anywhere, I know she's not a goddess. I know this magazine is wrong. Could you please show me the truth?"

My prayer was to be answered, as Mary patiently guided me back to the garden of faith.

Chapter Twelve
Two More Signs

Shortly after my return to California another sign appeared. There on the magazine stand at my local supermarket was *Life* magazine, July 1991, with a photograph of a statue of Our Lady on the cover, and beside the image in bold type, the question, "Do you believe in miracles?" My first fear was that *Life* had accepted the idea that the Virgin Mary was a goddess from heaven come down to earth. I picked up a copy, and to my relief, saw that the reporters had a different story to tell. The article listed all the places where Blessed Mother had recently appeared around the world and the contemporary miracles attributed to her. There were many.

I read every word in the article, and said to myself, "I must go to Yugoslavia." Finances and child care and other family issues made traveling there almost impossible, but these obstacles could be overcome. I still believed I could create the circumstances necessary for the trip, and began to pray my best manifesting prayer. I was determined to bring this trip, which existed only in my hopes, onto the material plane through the power of my own will. I prayed and prayed. It didn't occur to me then that I could pray with faith in God, that I could pray the rosary, and that the Holy Spirit would lead me where I needed to go.

As I waited for a trip to Medjugorje to materialize, I

encountered another sign. Every Sunday evening one of the women at the Teachings of the Inner Christ would host table-tipping sessions at the center in Lemon Grove. It was a way of attracting new people to the community, and on many Sundays you could find me there at the table. We would call upon the ascended masters, and different spirits would come into the space through us. They would show themselves mainly by moving objects around. Sometimes pianos were literally lifted off the floor before our eyes and transported across the room. People came from all over to watch and participate in these evenings of necromancy.

One evening, as I rested my hands on the table waiting for the entrance of some spirit guide or ascended master, I felt the unmistakable presence of something different, something next to me that was very beautiful, very angelic, very wonderful. I pulled my hands back at once from the table, and was unable to extend them again. It was as if they were locked against my body. After a moment, I stood up and left the room. Finding myself alone outside I asked, "What is this? Tell me what is happening."

An inner voice answered back, "I am the Queen of Peace."

I had never heard of the Queen of Peace, but I knew without question that it was Blessed Mother. The desire to know her, to learn about her immaculate heart, was continuing to sprout inside me. I said in response, "I'll never go back there."

My progress toward conversion began to move forward

at a faster pace after that. Already I was beginning to understand that there was something wrong with the path I was following. I wasn't supposed to be table-tipping or doing any of this ascended master stuff. Blessed Mother had delivered me from that table and that Center. She was leading me on to her son, Jesus.

Chapter Thirteen

Miraculous Medal

Within weeks of my table tipping experience, my grandmother passed away. I returned to the Seattle area for her funeral, and in the days that followed everything in her grand, old home was packed up and carried away.

The evening before I was to fly back to San Diego my mother and I did a final walkthrough of the empty house. As I took one last look through my grandmother's bedroom I noticed a shiny piece of jewelry lying on a countertop across the room all by itself. I thought, "How strange! How could we have missed this?" All the antiques and books and everything else had been cleared out, but this one piece of jewelry was left behind, the only thing, perhaps, belonging to my grandmother remaining in the entire house.

I walked over and picked up the necklace, held it up to my eyes and looked at it very carefully. Suspended from a delicate chain was a gold, oval-shaped medal with tiny writing around the edge. In the middle was a beautiful image of Blessed Mother extending her arms. At that moment I didn't know it was a Miraculous Medal. I just knew that my grandmother had always worn it. I was missing her so much, and I said to myself, "If it was important to her, it's important to me. I'll remember my grandmother whenever I wear it." It occurred to me that this might be the most valuable thing she could have left me.

So many things were to happen because of this medal. I put it on that evening, and since then have worn it always, even to this day.

Chapter Fourteen
The Crystal and the Rosary

One Monday evening a few weeks after my table-tipping experience, as I walked with Malia to her CCD class, I happened to notice a beautiful picture of the village of Medjugorje posted outside the church office. I went in and asked if someone from the church was planning to go there.

"One of the nuns just took a group from the parish," the receptionist said. She gave me the nun's name, and later that evening I called her. The nun gave me only a little information, and seemed reluctant to give more. I was intimidated enough not to bother her further, especially since I wasn't a practicing Catholic. Although I was hungry to learn more, I didn't know where to look or who else to ask.

It was a few weeks later when a New Age minister friend called one afternoon and told me to turn on the television. "The Joan Rivers show," she said, "has these priests* on who are talking about Medjugorje. They're showing rosaries that have changed from silver to gold. There's a woman with them from Arizona who channels Mother Mary. I remember you talking about this Catholic stuff, so I wanted to tell you. You really should see this."

I don't usually watch daytime television and was in the middle of a busy day, but I stopped what I was doing and

---

* The guests were Father Ken Roberts, author Michael Brown and Estella Ruiz.

tuned in. Sure enough, I called my friend afterwards and said, "Wow, this is interesting. We've got to find out more. Maybe there's a book. They'll know more at a bookstore, or maybe they can connect us with people who do."

It just happened that my daughter's babysitter was there, and she overheard our conversation. She said, "My mother works at the Catholic Charismatic Center in La Jolla. She can probably help you."

The girl called her mother, who invited us to come down to La Jolla and take a look. "We have lots of books, and there are several people here who have made pilgrimages to Med-jugorje."

The next morning I picked up my friend and we drove to La Jolla. While we were at this bookstore, we picked out a couple of books, looked at the jewelry and asked a lot of questions. "We want to know more about these appearances of Mother Mary. We saw this great show on TV. We really don't know anything. What can you tell us?"

One of the women working there had an idea: "We're going to have Bible study here Friday night. Why don't you join us?"

It was perfect timing. That Friday a man addressed the group who had just returned from Medjugorje. One of the negatives on his roll of film produced a print that showed a perfect white-cloud image of Our Lady against a background of blue sky. He explained that he had taken a picture of the Medjugorje landscape, and the image had only appeared when his film was developed back in California. He had copies of this print and he gave one to each of us. It was pretty inspiring.

After the man was finished and had sat down a woman went to the front of the room and started talking about the Bible. We thought, "Well, these people, they don't really know anything about the Bible. We have the inside story about the secret truths, the Gnostic teachings, the lost books," and so forth. It was definitely our time to split. "We're outta here, we gotta go." We were not interested.

We thought we'd go down to the beach, look at our new books and consult our spirit guides. As we hustled out the door of the Charismatic Center, this smiling older woman passed us going in the other direction. She looked at us and said "Where are you two going? Is the meeting over?"

We said, "It's over for us. We just came to find out about Medjugorje. We got this wonderful picture. Would you like to see it? Here it is. Now they're getting into the Bible and we're not interested. We're headed to the beach to do some prayers. We're going to manifest a trip to Medjugorje."

This lady, a complete stranger, informed us, "You don't need to go all the way to Medjugorje."

"What are you talking about? Of course we do. We want to see Mother Mary."

She said, "You can go to Scottsdale, Arizona, to the Church of Saint Maria Goretti."

We asked, "Where's that?"

"Well, it's right next to Phoenix, and you can drive there in six hours."

We thought, "That's a good deal. We don't even need to get on an airplane."

So, here we are, finding out for the first time about apparitions of Mother Mary in Scottsdale. We asked, "Do you mean they are actually channeling Mary?"

A devout Catholic, the woman was not quite sure what we meant by "channeling." She said "Well, um, yes. I suppose so. We call it 'locution.' On Thursday evenings they say the rosary and have Mass, and then Blessed Mother appears and gives a message. There's a beautiful little chapel, and a lot of other wonderful things are happening there."

She wrote down the name of the church, the directions, everything we needed to know.

We thought, "This is great!" and after thanking the stranger we headed to the beach.

At the time I had no idea that this woman, Beverly Nelson, a lay Missionary of Charity in Mother Teresa's order, would have a tremendous influence on my life in the years that followed.

As soon as we got to the beach, we sat down in the sand and pulled out our crystals. All good New Agers keep their crystals with them so that they can receive messages from their higher self with the help of spirit guides. I know it may sound strange to get advice from a rock, but that's the way we all thought back then. The crystals are attached to the end of a chain. When they are held out like a pendulum, they communicate through the way they move. My friend held out her crystal and started to ask for advice but, strangely, it hung perfectly still in the ocean breeze. It wouldn't budge. So my friend said to me, "You're better at this than I am. Why don't you try it? Ask a question."

I reached out to take the pendulum, but in the middle of its motion my hand was literally stopped. It was as if there was an impenetrable barrier between the pendulum and me. As I looked down to see what was blocking my hand, I saw that a beautiful white rosary had been draped over it. In the same moment I heard a voice within me saying clearly, "Only the rosary. Pray the rosary. Through prayer, all is answered."

I wouldn't call this experience a miracle. I hadn't come into the Church yet but I was still clairvoyant. I was still seeing continuously into the psychic realm. The Lord uses all things for His good and His glory.

As I looked at my hand I said, "Oh my gosh. I need to pray the rosary."

Then I looked up at my friend and told her, "I'm not allowed to touch that crystal. Mother Mary has just told me to get a rosary. I need to pray the rosary, and she'll answer my prayers. I can't use crystals any more, ever."

My friend knew I was telling the truth. She knew I was clairvoyant and had seen this proven many times. She got very excited.

"Do you think they make rosaries out of crystals?" she wondered aloud.

Chapter Fifteen

"I Am Your Mother"

Little more than a month had passed since the episode at the beach when I gathered together a carload of New Agers and headed for Scottsdale. I was so excited by what happened there that I made seven such trips within the next six months. I took dozens of friends and many of them shared my excitement. That's how powerfully Our Lady touched us. It was so beautiful.

Our first trip there was planned as a stopover on the way to Sedona. We arrived at St. Maria Goretti Church just in time for the Thursday evening Mass. The service that night was a combination healing Mass and witnessing of the Marian apparition. In preparation for the trip I had decided to fast. I hadn't eaten for 24 hours, and I had been praying and praying to Jesus and Mary to help me be receptive. When we entered the church, it was standing room only. The rosary was just beginning, and my friends looked around and decided they were not interested. They went back outside, while I took the stairs up to the balcony, which was less crowded, where I found a seat.

As I looked out over the congregation, I didn't notice anything special about the nine young people in the front row, but when they did the rosary, during the third mystery, one of the women seated there had a locution. She was one of the visionaries. She didn't communicate the message to anyone else right then, but you could see her writing things down. Then during the homily — I didn't understand these things until later, after several trips — the priest also received messages from Mary. Many of these were eventually published as the "I Am Your Jesus of Mercy" series. I think there are more than a dozen of these books available.

Just after the homily the priest, Father Jack Spaulding, approached the altar, bowed his head, closed his eyes and established himself in a deep calm. Then he began to speak words that were not his own, words that seemed to come directly from Mary:

> My dear little children, praise be to Jesus! I am your Mother of Joy, who so desires you to live in the world in peace, though peace does not exist, since there is division. There is division because of the conflict, which exists in the values of the world. My little, little children, do not alter your standards of following the Gospel in order to satisfy the needs of others. Never deviate from the truth of His Word. You do not please Him by jeopardizing your freedom living deceitful ways of life. The only way to freedom is by living the truth outlined by my Son. He has given you His Word. You cannot change His words and live dishonest lives and see that peace exists. There is only one way. That way is the way of my Son in His Word in the Gospel. He is your God. There is only one God. I plead with you that you hold fast to His Word, not to deviate from the stance on truth or you will suffer tremendously at the hands of man. I love you, my little ones, and bless you. I desire you to be happy and free. You must return to God and the truth

of His Word. Killings of all sorts, greed, abuse, selfish-
ness, anger, malice, dishonesty, adultery and other sexual
disgraces, those of children, men and women, are vices
which prevent your freedom. Reconcile your sins and
live in His truth. Thank you for responding to my call.
Ad Deum.

That first evening I was deeply disturbed at what I saw
and heard. I had come all the way from San Diego to see Our
Lady and to have a direct experience of her presence, and now
I see this priest going into what looked like New Age chan-
neling. I was, in fact, upset and confused and I said to myself,
"What is this priest doing? I don't understand this. Has the
New Age infiltrated the Catholic Church this much? I might
as well stick with the New Agers."

I was just so surprised and shocked. And then I stood
up, closed my eyes and prayed in my heart, "Lord Jesus, if this
priest is from you, give me a sign, otherwise I'm leaving this
church and I'm never coming back."

I opened my eyes, and right then and there, superim-
posed over the face of Father Spaulding as he stood at the
altar, I saw the image of Jesus' face in his Passion. He wore the
crown of thorns on his head and blood was dripping down.
In that same instant I heard an interior voice saying, "This is
my son. He is my disciple. Sit down. You are home."

The authority of this inner voice was so strong I sat
down. I couldn't leave. I stayed there through that Mass, shared
the Eucharist with deep emotion, and watched the healing
session afterwards. I, who had been a healer for many years,

saw for the first time the awesome healing power of the Holy Spirit in action. The impact of this experience is more than I could ever put into words.

When the service was over I knew that I needed to get to confession immediately. I mean, *immediately.* I hadn't been to confession since the age of fifteen!

As I walked out into the parking lot, I spotted someone there who looked like they knew their way around the church. I went up to him, a complete stranger, and said, "Excuse me, sir. I need confession right away. Can you help me find a priest?"

The man answered, "Go look in the sacristy. He's probably still there."

I didn't know what or where the sacristy was, so I hurried around outside the church, looking everywhere, thinking, "He's got to be here somewhere. I've got to find him."

All of a sudden there he was, Father Spaulding, coming out of the back of the church and walking out to his car. As he was getting ready to leave, I came up to him and said, "Father, I need confession right now."

"Here, in the parking lot?"

"If you don't mind."

So people are walking by, talking in groups, starting their cars, slamming their doors, driving off. The priest probably figured I was a local Catholic that needed a quick confession for some venial sin. I began by saying, "Father, I don't remember how to start. How do I do this?"

And he says, "You know: 'Bless me Father for I have sinned. It has been so much time since my last confession.'"

I responded, "Bless me Father for I have sinned. It has been twenty-five years since my last confession," and his jaw actually dropped. It's late, it's dark and a little cold, we're in the parking lot standing next to his open car door, cars are driving by out on the street and idling at the traffic lights. He wasn't ready for this. But he could see how earnest I was so he went ahead with it.

During that first, thirty-minute-long, parking lot confession my passage back to the Faith opened wide. There would be no turning back the conversion process. When we were finished, I thanked Father Spaulding and went off excitedly to find my friends. The first place I looked was the adoration chapel.

The adoration chapel at St. Maria Goretti Church is a special place. My New Age friends had found their way there while I attended Mass. They stayed there meditating before the Blessed Sacrament for nearly four hours that day. They didn't know anything about the presence of Jesus. They just knew the chapel was a place of peace and silence, and they were touched. One of my friends, Gary, was a musician and he actually heard the voice of Our Lady. All of the songs that he sang for the rest of the week, as we traveled from Scottsdale to Sedona and back to California, were devotional songs to Our Lady, and they were beautiful.

In the adoration chapel, while my friends silently meditated, I prayed to Our Lady, thanking her and asking her for guidance. We remained there together for over two hours, then it was time to go. It was getting late and we still had a long drive ahead of us. As I prepared to leave I actually felt a little disappointment. Since our arrival in Scottsdale I hadn't heard the voice of Our Lady directly. In the adoration chapel I had felt the presence of holiness. I felt powerfully drawn to the space and did not want to leave. But it was not until I opened the door to leave that I clearly heard Our Lady speak to me, inside my heart. She said, simply, "I am your mother."

At the sound of those words I broke down in tears. It was a conviction so deep. I answered her, "I'll be back,"

We drove on to Sedona that night and I continued to cry tears of joy and gratitude. Our Lady had reached out to me to show me how much she loved me, and her love and presence never left me as we journeyed on across the high, darkened desert.

Chapter Sixteen
The Prince of Peace

My musician friend, Gary, who joined us on that first trip to Scottsdale, had followed a Hindu teacher for about fifteen years. From our many hours of talking and learning together about gurus, and also about UFOs and other New Age phenomena, we had built a fast friendship. A few weeks after our trip he noticed the Miraculous Medal I was wearing. He was fascinated, because for a long time I had only worn crystals. He, too, had always worn a serious crystal around his neck.

He asked me, "Why are you wearing this necklace? What happened to your crystal?"

By then I had learned more about the history of the Miraculous Medal, so I told him the story — about St. Catherine Labouré and her visions and the power that people attributed to it. Then I said, "I've got to go and buy Christmas presents this afternoon. This year I've decided to do all of my holiday shopping at this Catholic gift shop. It's at Mission San Luis Rey in Oceanside. There's an amazing old mission church there. Would you like to come along?"

I thought he would say, "No, of course not." Instead he said, "Yeah, I'll come."

As we headed north from my house, I said to Gary, "Anything in the store you want, I'll buy it for you for Christmas."

Well, I didn't think he'd find anything there, but it turns

out he wanted to have the biggest and most expensive sterling silver Miraculous Medal in the store.

I said, "No problem. I'll get it for you."

When we left the gift shop we walked over to see the chapel. Mission San Luis Rey has a gorgeous enclosed garden, densely planted with trees and vines, with a statue of Our Lady and dozens of rose bushes of every variety. For centuries, people have prayed on these grounds. God's blessings are apparent in the singing birds and lush greenery, and a spirit of sanctity hangs in the air. On our way to the chapel we followed the stone path through the leaves.

Gary said, "You know, I feel such peace here. It's really . . . It must be very holy ground. Why don't I take off my crystal and put this medal on."

I got a call from Gary about a week later "You know, that Mother of yours must be talking to me. I need to pray the rosary. Do you know anything about it? Where can I get a rosary?"

Gary was the person who introduced me to another favorite holy place: Prince of Peace Abbey, a Benedictine monastery, also in Oceanside. In a quest for the perfect rosary, Gary discovered this dramatic mountaintop retreat by word of mouth, and started to go there to hear the monks praying the Divine Office and offering Mass. He was aware that in my movement away from the New Age and toward Jesus, I had become subject to especially strong psychic assaults. Although I had begun to find peace in reciting the rosary and in prayer, this quietness of mind was impossible to sustain. I continued to see movies in my head of people's lives, their past experiences, and these visions were becoming increasingly disturbing. They kept me awake at night to the point that I was continually drained.

So Gary calls me one day — he wasn't even a Catholic at this point — and he says, "I want to take you for a ride somewhere." When I asked where, he just said it was a surprise, and that it would be do me good.

He picked me up and we headed to Oceanside. Following the freeway as it turned eastward, we took an exit into one of the grassy valleys that cover the north county area. As we wound down a deserted road there I saw a little, hand-painted sign with the words, "Prince of Peace." And I thought, "Hmmm?" And I said to Gary, "Who's the Prince of Peace?" I was thinking it must be some Franciscan saint with a shrine left over from the mission days. Something like that, I didn't really know. And he said, "Are you really that dumb? Didn't you ever go to Sunday school? Don't you have any memory of anything? Didn't you know that's a name for Jesus — Prince of Peace?"

"I'm sorry. I don't remember. I guess I never learned that one."

"Well, I believe it says somewhere in the Gospels that Jesus gives a peace that no man can give. It's a beyond-this-world kind of peace."

"I could sure use that. I have no peace at all, and I need it really bad."

As we arrived, midday Mass was about to begin. The monks filed into the church and began to sing. It all seemed a little medieval. I wasn't quite comfortable, and most of the time I wasn't sure exactly what was going on. There were all of these priests at the altar doing things, saying things, and I just sat there. Finally I lowered my head in prayer and said, "Lord, if you offer a peace that's beyond this world, and if it's your will, I accept it. My friend here tells me that you give a peace that no man can give, and that is what I seek."

Sure enough, by the end of that Mass I had felt a very deep peace come over me, a peace greater than any I had felt in my entire life. It was perfectly silent inside me, inexpressible in words. I remained in the pew after Mass ended, and prayed quietly until it began to grow dark outside. I couldn't leave. I couldn't move. I didn't want to interrupt that peace.*

When I got home that night I found the sound of the radio and television, even the telephone ringing, shrill and irritating. I carried with me a gift of tranquility that I didn't want to relinquish. Anyone in the psychic or clairvoyant business, I can promise you, would love to have that. So, as I've written before, they're the first to evangelize. I challenge everyone to go talk to a psychic. Pick the most accomplished case, and you will find that person the most ripe for conversion.

---

* Later in my walk with Christ, I found my Spiritual Director, Fr. David, at Prince of Peace Abbey. Fr. David would lead me through a three-year program called Healing of Memories. This program is based on the work of the Claretian priest and author, Fr. John Hampsch.

Chapter Seventeen
Housecleaning

Going to Mass, spiritual reading and prayer were now the foundations of my conversion process. I read about Mother Teresa of Calcutta, who emphasized the message "to Jesus through Mary." Mother Teresa's teachings encouraged me to consecrate every day to Mary's Immaculate Heart and to continue wearing the Miraculous Medal with devotion. I studied St. Louis Mary de Montfort's books on the rosary, and did a forty-day meditation that he had written. To do that was a great practice for me. I learned by heart the prayers of St. Michael the Archangel and St. Benedict, prayers designed to loosen the grip of Satan, and recited them periodically throughout the day. Those prayers, for me, seemed to say it all. The spirits of the New Age had sought the ruin of my soul. I knew that firsthand, and with their help I was fighting back. I also fasted at least one day per week, sometimes several days in a row.

In all these efforts I was certain that Blessed Mother was interceding for me, just as she had promised. Through God's grace, she led me to the mother of one of Malia's friends, who invited me to join a Bible study group. This wonderful woman was determined to pick me up every Thursday morning and take me to their meeting. She was perfectly steadfast, persuading me to accompany her every week, whether I resisted or made excuses or didn't feel like it or whatever. She stayed strong. That was really beautiful of her, to make that sacrifice and put up with my confusion.

I remember the first day I attended this class and heard these enthusiastic charismatic Catholics talking about humans as "creatures of the Creator." I thought, "Isn't that strange? Don't these people realize that they really don't have to think that way? They really can be co-creators." Then there was another lesson: "The day that we discover we are not God is the day we begin our conversion experience." This line seemed to speak directly to me, but still I found it too naive to accept.

So I kept going to that Bible class even though I didn't fully understand or agree with everything they were saying. From the Course in Miracles and the New Thought churches I had learned that thoughts in the mind are relative; they're not real. Our minds can be enlightened through certain practices and meditations. We can become "self-realized," and we certainly do not need to be redeemed from anything called sin. Even at this point I wasn't completely convinced that I needed a savior. I did know, however, that I needed to keep going to Bible study. The people there embodied so much love and humility and peacefulness in their lives that I couldn't help but see them as role models. I strongly desired to know the word of God as they did, to have what they had. Their way of life became my goal.

My next challenge was to clear out all my New Age books and other paraphernalia. I wasn't strong enough yet in my faith to do it myself, but I probably never would be until all these objects and influences were gone from my life. Along with their prayers and fasting and uncompromising support, this was another way in which my Bible study contacts were to help free me from bondage.

At first the leader of the group came to my house and walked through all the rooms, pointing out the objects that needed to go. It was like Deuteronomy, chapter 7, where God tells his people to destroy all the pagan objects they find when they reach the promised land; or Acts, chapter 19, where the followers of Paul at Ephesus burn their occult books, which they value at 50,000 silver pieces. I threw away much of what she told me to dispose of, but a lot of it I kept. I was still attached to these objects in ways I could not explain.

This woman had to come several times and take things away herself, but still I was helpless to complete the job. Finally another lay friend from a local charismatic ministry, Tom, came over with his station wagon to physically remove and dump every last piece of New Age paraphernalia. The work took several days. I had thousands and thousands of dollars worth of occult objects in my house: books, audio tapes, videos, icons, statues, jewelry, clothing, meditation cushions, sacred shawls and plants, candles, lots of pagan ritual objects. My collection of UFO photos and videos was probably one of the larger ones in the country. And I had crystals — crystal balls, crystal necklaces and rings, display crystals, very expensive crystal pendulums, and chunks of amethyst and quartz programmed for esoteric purposes. These were not just nice-looking gems, but stones into which specific dark forces had been called by name in order to perform occult tasks.

I had such a hard time doing this, I know now, because I hadn't yet been delivered from the demons connected with these objects. So when this gentle and supportive Christian man came to deliver my home from all this stuff, I actually became physically ill. I had an overpowering resistance to him removing things from my house, which all but paralyzed me. He would pick up a book and say, "What's this book about? Is this part of the occult?"

And when I said, "Yes," he would say, "Get rid of it."

He came out to help me like Mother Teresa coming to serve the poor. It was a great act of mercy mainly because he had to deal with my reactions, which were irrational and hostile. At one point, when he picked up my copy of *A Course in Miracles*, the greatest bible I had known for the previous twenty years of my life, I was so devastated by the thought of letting go that I lost control. I hadn't the strength or the will to finally and utterly reject this set of teachings.

I only know from being told afterward that I began screaming nonsense, or rather, demons attached to the Course in Miracles began screaming through me. Tom was stunned by my reaction. He turned away and ceased to reason with me. He calmly took every last book off the shelf, placed them all in a big black garbage bag and carried them out into the back yard. Then he came back, took me by the hand and led me outside. He prayed over me, and then we sat down and sifted through the bag, taking out each book one at a time and deciding whether it should be kept or had to go. Neither I nor Tom will ever forget that.

This clearing of the house was a major work of deliverance, carried out by two gifted laypeople. Even though these charismatic Catholics had no formal credentials in deliverance, they realized that attending Mass, sitting in at RCIA classes and going to Bible study would not be enough to free me of my past if every day I came home to a space that was contaminated. They knew from their Bible reading, and through the power of the Holy Spirit, that my home had to be cleared of idols.

When our work was finally complete, the only thing I didn't dispose of was my collection of UFO videos. They were given to Michael Brown, the Christian author of *Trumpets of Gabriel,* for his research on the possible connection between UFOs and the demonic world. Everything else went to the dump. Still, as I was soon to discover, one more thing in my life had to be thoroughly cleared of the traces of idolatry. That was me. I still had to clear out me.

Chapter Eighteen
Both Sides of the Fence

For a couple of years, from the time of my first trip to Scottsdale to my pilgrimage to Medjugorje, the flower of my Christian devotion grew slowly but steadily. I wouldn't say that I ever took a step backward toward my New Age world, but my discernment was far from perfect.

One day, for example, a friend from the Bible study group loaned me a tape of Father Richard Thomas, a charismatic Catholic priest from El Paso, Texas. He's pretty incredible. I was very impressed by this tape because Fr. Thomas talked about the power of the Holy Spirit, and indeed, New Age churches talk about the Holy Spirit, too. What wasn't clear to me, was that these are not the same spirit — not at all — and in my pride, I thought perhaps I could actually reconcile these two seemingly opposing faiths: New Thought and Catholicism.

A few days later, as I was driving up Interstate 5 listening to Father Thomas, I heard him describe some of his experiences helping the poor in Juarez, Mexico. He said that somehow, no matter what level of poverty or what level of need they faced, they never ran short of food. Somehow they always had on hand enough beans and rice and sandwiches and fruit to feed the hungry. He called this occurrence "multiplication," and described several incidents where food was served

that clearly exceeded the amount that his workers had prepared.

I turned my car around and headed back toward the
Church of Religious Science. There was someone there who
needed to hear this. When I arrived, the minister and I sat
down together and listened to Father Thomas' story. When
he was finished I turned to her and said, "Isn't this amazing?
Here is a Catholic priest who is actually manifesting!"

Almost the moment these words came out of my mouth
I could feel the error in what I was saying. The look in her
eyes told me she probably had a similar feeling. It became
clear to me right then that what Father Thomas had described
had almost nothing in common with the techniques of manifestation I had learned at the Church of Religious Science. In
the first place, Father Thomas was *praying to God* that God's
will be done, and he was praying that *if it be God's will* the poor
people in his care be fed. I had always been taught that *I* was
the manifestor, and that *my success* in creating reality depended
on the strength and purity of *my will*. God was not part of the
equation, and selfless charity was pretty much never the solution I worked toward.

As I left there that afternoon, I was unable to put these
conflicting thoughts into words, but the minister said to me,
"You know Moira, I was raised Catholic also. I think most of
our congregation was." This comment has been food for
thought in the years since.

Somehow this experience at the Church of Religious Science is related in my thinking to something that happened about the same time on the Catholic side of the fence.

It says in Leviticus, chapter 19, "Do not go to mediums or consult fortune-tellers, because you will be defiled by them." Psychics, spirit guides, spiritual advisers, clairvoyants — these are all contemporary terms for the kind of occult professionals that the Lord was referring to in this passage. In spite of His warning, many Christians consult with mediums and fortune-tellers to this day. Sometimes they even invite them into the Church.

Some Filipino neighbors, dear friends of mine, were very happy about my return to the faith. One day they invited me to join them at a special Mass, an annual holiday in the local Filipino community, after which there would be a speaker from the Philippines, someone with great spiritual gifts

After what was a lovely Mass — the room was filled with devotion to Jesus and Mary — a woman from the Philippines was introduced, someone who called herself "Sister" with a capital S. This, I knew, is not allowed in the Church unless a person has taken religious vows. This woman was married with children.

The host of the event introduced her as a "trance medium." He explained that she would lie down, and Jesus as a baby boy would speak to us through her. All of us were welcome to come up to her and ask her anything we wanted or request special favors, and there would surely be no delay in having our prayers answered.

I had seen this same performance before in the New Age business many times. Although in some ways it resembled the experience of what the Church calls "locution," which I had witnessed at St. Maria Goretti Church, it was clear to me that this had to be the work of a psychic spirit, not the Holy Spirit. It was a display of power rather than a call to love. People were motivated by the prospect of having their wishes fulfilled, rather than by a sense of surrender to God's will.

I thought, "What? What a great deal! Our own Christian medium! Our own Catholic magician!"

I looked around at all the excited faces. I knew what they were feeling and thinking, and I knew they were responding to a spirit that was not to be trusted.

"This is not okay," I said to my friends. "Haven't you read about this in the Bible? I studied this kind of thing for years. The Church is no place for a trance medium. I've got to leave."

I got up and walked out, waiting in the church garden until the end of the service. My friends, I am sorry to say, were offended and felt very uncomfortable around me for nearly a year. In the end, however, they came to recognize that this Sister was not legitimate.

Christians need to be vigilant. Jesus is continually being mimicked and mocked by his archenemy. Even in the Church — if not especially in the Church — this is dangerous stuff.

Chapter Nineteen
Deliverance at Medjugorje

Although I was now a devout practicing Catholic I was still affected by the New Age. Clearing out my house, attending Mass, going to confession every Saturday, praying the rosary: These were important steps, but they were only preparation for fully receiving Jesus Christ as my savior. I knew this. My stubborn resistance to much of what I was hearing in Bible study, and the confusion and anxiety that assailed me, less frequently than before, but still often, showed me that the journey back to faith was not yet finished.

Looking back, I am not surprised. I had so far to go! All the thought systems of my youth had been washed away. The file cards in my brain that were once labeled "Judeo-Christian belief" had been erased and written over with New Age lies. The Evil One still tempted me, for example, with false proofs of reincarnation. This was one of the most difficult heresies for me to reject. Many others I preserved in my heart, believing that they were not, after all, so very important. I assumed that I would never need to face up to them in the confessional, or if I did, that I could say a few words and that would be the end of it. I didn't know that each of these lingering lies were blocks against my complete deliverance, that there was no way out for me other than to open my heart, to read aloud the name on each file card one by one and renounce it. To recognize this necessity and guide me across this last river into the arms of Jesus would require a very special priest.

During the military conflicts in Croatia in the late 1990s, I was an international godparent to child victims of the war. I donated money to help support some young refugees, who were safely cared for on an island off the Balkan coast. In 1996 I traveled with a group of pilgrims to that island in order to meet my godchildren in person, to learn what else might be done to help them. Shortly after we reached the refugee community, we decided as a group to visit Medjugorje, to see the place where Blessed Mother was still appearing daily and to worship at St. James Church. At last I had made it to Medjugorje, without prayers of manifestation, through the workings of the Holy Spirit.

On the day of our arrival I settled into our hotel, then walked across the village to the church. I wanted to have confession before evening Mass. Hundreds of pilgrims had the same idea. They were queued up outside the confessional booths, each of which was dedicated to speakers of a different language. In the English line fifty or sixty people waited patiently. It was the longest line — that day only one booth was available to English speakers. I took my place at the end of the line and stood there for two hours in the baking heat of August, recalling to mind all the sins I had committed over the past week.

When at last I took my seat in the confessional, I told the priest a few things about myself. When I mentioned that I had been involved in the New Age before my recent conversion, his response took me by surprise "Oh, no! All the New

Agers come to me. If you're New Age you end up here in my confessional."

His response was so spontaneous, spoken with such warmth and understanding, that I was moved to tell him far more than the venial sins I had committed. I gradually began to reveal to him bits and pieces of my background in the occult. One story led to another. I told him many things I had never told a priest before, and I told him I was still suffering.

The confessor I had chanced upon, it turns out, was Father Philip Pavich, O.S.F. Father Philip, I learned later, was a Franciscan who had served for many years in Israel before being transferred to Medjugorje. He was sent there because of his extraordinary gift for healing confession. That was his charism.

My confession that afternoon lasted two-and-a-half hours and would have lasted longer, but the situation was getting rather outrageous. Sixty people or more were still lined up outside, most of whom had been waiting for hours. I told Father Philip I felt bad about that, but he told me not to worry. He knew exactly what to do.

"What you are describing is not middle-of-the-road New Age. You have gone deeply into the occult. There is much more to be done. We need to stop now, but if you want to finish what we have started, I would like you to meet me at my office tomorrow. We have deliverance work to do.

"If you are to be set free from the demons that attack you, we must go through all of your occult experiences together. Come see me in the rectory tomorrow."

The next morning, immediately after Mass, I went to St. James rectory. There I was greeted by Father Philip, whom I was meeting face to face for the first time. The day before, he had been concealed by the curtain in the confessional. Father Philip was an older man with grey hair, strongly built, of medium height. He wore the coarse brown habit of a Franciscan monk, with a stole draped over his shoulders, which priests wear when they give the sacrament of reconciliation.

His office was on the main floor of the rectory. It seemed to me to be a very holy space. It was well lit, with a bright sun shining through white curtains casting long shadows. The room was large enough to hold a medium-sized desk with two chairs facing it, shelves along the walls filled with books in half a dozen languages, and a group of more comfortable chairs off to the side, where Father Philip did his spiritual counseling. He and I sat down across from each other there. On the wall above his head hung a large silver cross with what appeared to be a reliquary built into it.

Father Philip told me we what were going to go do: He wanted me to tell him every practice — that's the word he used: "practice" — I had ever done in the occult. He needed to know what I had learned, who my teachers were, and who the spirits were that I had invoked. He had to know every-thing, without exception, and I was to specifically and de-voutly renounce each and every practice. The gravity with which Father Philip spoke frightened me a little, but it also encour-aged me to trust him completely. He said he was going to "pick me clean."

I started from the beginning. I confessed to Father Philip my early religious skepticism and experience in meditation, my search for a guru, my infatuation with success, and then recounted my accident and all the involvements that followed upon it. The session was to last over fourteen hours, all one day and most of the next. We only stopped to eat, rest, and, of course, he had his duties as a priest to attend to. Although it was a traumatic experience, it was also ultimately liberating. Even now as I recall it, I am moved to tears.

As I recited the litany of my occult involvements, Father Philip listened and prayed. He knew exactly what prayers to say. I was usually unable to hear his exact words, nor did I feel the need to. I had surrendered my will and continued to confess, uninterrupted, with deep repentance and great faith. After every practice I confessed, Father Philip commanded me to formally renounce it, its teachers and its attending spirits in the name of Jesus Christ. It was not enough for me simply to say, "I did these things," as if this were some Catholic version of psychoanalysis. A total, formal, remorseful rejection of each practice was demanded of me. In this way, hesitantly and often with painful resistance, I rejected every school, every teacher and every spirit I had ever worked with.

There were many things I could not remember about my past. My time in the New Age was long and my memory was imperfect. But whatever I was unable to recall Father Philip provided. The Holy Spirit had granted him the gift of knowledge, and as a result he knew the names and histories of every demon that had afflicted me. He knew my relationships with them better than I knew them myself. I was reminded of Padre Pio, who was aware of the sins of his petitioners in confession even when they neglected to mention them. People would begin their confession and he would finish it for them.

In the 1970s, for example, I had studied EST, a method of "self-actualization." When I mentioned EST I couldn't remember the name of the man who had inspired this movement. Father Philip provided the name: Werner Erhard. The same thing happened when I mentioned firewalking, which I had practiced with Anthony Robbins. I forgot Robbins' name but Father Philip supplied it. He rebuked aloud the spirits that guided these teachings with formal prayers, as I renounced their presence in my life.

I told him I had practiced channeling and Reiki, and in the name of Jesus and by the power of the Holy Spirit he delivered me from the demons of these activities. He called out their names, names I knew, and I saw more clearly than ever how every occult practice has a demon attached to it.

In the Gospels [John 4,4] there is a story about a woman Jesus met at a well. Although she was a stranger, Jesus told this woman the story of her life. She offered him water from the well and, in exchange, he offered her the living water of the Word. That's what it was like for me. It was like being with Jesus. Father Philip knew my life story, and in exchange for making room for God in my heart with deep repentance I was given the purifying, life-giving water of Jesus.

The list of unholy pretenders whom Father Philip ordered me to renounce is long. When I mentioned psychic healing, Father Philip reminded me that Jack Schwarz was my teacher, which, of course, was correct. I had studied the science of human energy systems with him, and I renounced him that day. He knew of Barbara Brennan and her spirit guide, Heyoan, and commanded me to renounce those two as well.

I told him about my initiation by the Sikh guru Thakar Singh. I had forgotten the names of the other masters, Kirpal Singh and Sawan Singh, but Father Philip spoke their names and demanded that I renounce them. He reminded me of their appearance in my bedroom years earlier.

I told him that more than anything I wanted to close the third eye of clairvoyance. I didn't want to see psychic movies anymore. He ordered me to renounce this skill, to submit with all my heart my power of clairvoyance to the dispensation of God. Father Philip then declared that this would never bother me again. When I asked, "How do you know that?" he explained to me what the "gift of knowledge" and the "gift of deliverance" were. The Holy Spirit had granted him the ability to name demons, to see into the lives of the afflicted, and to invoke the Holy Spirit to set them free.

When I told him that I had practiced yoga, he began to recite the names of various yogic schools: Tantra, Hatha, Bhakti, Kundalini. I indicated those I had practiced and, where I could, named the teachers and spirit guides. I told him how Maharishi Mahesh Yogi, founder of Transcendental Meditation, had come to me in dreams. I mentioned homeopathy and he prompted me to renounce Samuel Hahnemann himself, the founder of that science. "We need to close the doors that homeopathy opened. Demons have been using them to reach you."

As a child I had played with a Ouija Board, and as an adult I had learned the I Ching, a Chinese divination tool. I had studied necromancy and tarot cards. These fortune-telling practices were named and renounced along with their patron spirits. I said the name José Silva, but was unable to connect him to any practice. Father Philip filled in the blank: the hypnosis practice called Silva Mind Control. I renounced it.

Father Philip had warned me that my deliverance might make me feel sick. That was true. Throughout all of the first day and most of the second I was terribly nauseous. At one point I told Father Philip about my experiences with the Course in Miracles. I had studied with Dr. William Thetford, one of the founders of the movement, a professional colleague of Dr. Helen Schucman, which I will write about later. During this session I actually started to babble unintelligibly, and was overcome with weakness. Dr. Philip laid hands upon me and prayed until the illness passed.

I was able to recall that I had a vision at the Summit Lighthouse Church in Malibu, but the details of that event were lost from my memory. When I said "Summit Lighthouse," Father Philip knew. "There was a so-called 'ascended master.' His name is El Morya. In Jesus' name, renounce him." I did so as he prayed.

One practice I have not mentioned yet is Native American shamanism. Years earlier I had participated in Medicine

Wheel ceremonies with a man named Sun Bear. These were elaborate, round-the-clock rituals held in the desert of Eastern Washington with native teachers, where we chanted and drummed and called upon the spirits of nature.

I had also studied Medicine Wheel philosophy and card divination with Jamie Sams, who has written a number of books on Native American religion. Sams teaches her followers how to work with animal guides. The idea is that each of us has our own unique spirit guide, who appears to us in the form of an animal. During a weekend retreat, Sams showed a group of us how to discover what that animal is and make contact with it. As she guided us in our efforts, my clairvoyance began to create difficulties. I kept seeing Sams' own animal guide. So here I am, the new kid in the class, and I say, "Ms. Sams, what is happening? I see your animal guide."

I told her what it was, and she responded, "You're right."

For the rest of that long weekend we spent together, Sams kept an eye on me. Eventually, as the other workshop participants began to discover their animal guides, I could see them all. The whole experience was very disturbing, and when my animal guide made his presence known after I had returned home, I wanted nothing to do with it. I told this story to Father Philip — a Catholic priest who had never, ever been involved in shamanism. He knew the entire story already.

Father Philip then asked me to go back and retrieve any esoteric practices that had been performed on me. In other words, if I had allowed anyone to perform rituals or apply occult techniques to me, then I was contaminated and needed to be cleansed. For example, although I knew nothing about the science of palm reading, I had my palm read many times.

"Where?" he asked.

"At the Institute of Mentalphysics."

"You will renounce that now, in Jesus' name. Renounce that you allowed yourself to have someone read your palm."

I had also visited a Dianetics institute. I was not interested in learning Dianetics — believe it or not — but I had one of the teachers walk me through a Dianetics session. That's all I knew about this system. I didn't even know the name of the person who taught this. Father Pavich knew, and he ordered me to renounce Dianetics and the teacher specifically by name.

In the midafternoon of the second day the ordeal was finished. There was nothing more to confess. I cannot say for certain that the experience was an exorcism. I do know, however, that it exceeded in power and effect anything I have witnessed in rituals of deliverance. I felt like a baby, a little baby who has new skin, as if someone had scrubbed me right down to the bone. Father Philip, as he had said, had picked me clean. I was a new creature, a newborn child in the family of God. I almost didn't know who I was. I didn't have an identity anymore, because who I used to be had been washed away, and who I was to become was too new. I had to hold Our Lady's hand to even stand up and walk away, to start on my path as a new creature in Christ. And I knew that I would never let go of that hand again.

Part Two

Stories of Conversion

Chapter One
A Deep Love for Souls

When I first returned to the Church I felt useless, as though I had thrown away my life. I thought, "I have wasted so many years looking for truth in the wrong places." But as Paul says in Romans, chapter 8, "All things work for good for those who love God." The Lord, I discovered, had the power to build something useful even from the scraps of my New Age history.

Early one morning, after a long night of soul-searching, I went to Mass. When the service ended I got on my knees and prayed with all my heart. "Lord, I know how much time I have wasted, but I ask you, please, do not let me waste another moment of my life. By your grace I have found peace. May this grace grow in me so that I might do your work. Show me what that work is, and I will try to do it."

I remember crying as I prayed, "Lord, I don't know how you can use me. I feel paralyzed. I have never served anyone but myself, and I want to change. How do I do that? I am only human. You are divine. Please take my human heart and help it to follow your will."

God answered my prayer by granting me a deep love for souls and a zeal to evangelize. I didn't need to go out and knock on doors with a Bible in my hand, or stand on a busy street corner passing out leaflets. He led me to people I knew who were receptive to the Lord's call.

Chapter Two
The Little Flower in Hawaii

Whenever I help someone toward conversion I feel that I am participating in the communion of saints. I feel that they are assisting me, particularly Blessed Teresa of Calcutta (best known as Mother Teresa) and her favorite saint and namesake, Saint Therese of Lisieux, the Little Flower. Saint Therese always said that she wanted to go out and evangelize the world, but her Carmelite vocation and poor health prevented her from doing so. I believe that in a mysterious way, she helps me to carry out her work. This story is an example:

A few weeks after my petition in the church, my daughter Malia and I went on a vacation to Hawaii. There, on a beautiful, uncrowded beach on the south shore of Maui, we said a very simple prayer that went something like this: "Lord, thank you for the gift of this vacation. But, if you or Our Lady would like us to serve you in some way while we are here, we give our time to you."

Whenever you say a heartfelt prayer, the Lord hears you. Sure enough, in a few days he found a job for us. We went to see an old friend who lived nearby. She was part of my New Age past, and we thought the Lord might use us to reach out to her. During our first visit, we didn't have a chance to talk about religious matters, but my friend introduced us to her roommate, Emily, a woman in her fifties, who was not feeling well. The next morning as I prayed for Emily's recovery I was inspired to go back and see her again.

Malia and I went to my friend's house and talked with Emily for a while. Then we decided to go with my friend and her son to the beach, do some snorkeling, have a picnic and enjoy the day. I expected that once we were at the beach, I could speak to my friend and talk to her about my new life in Christ. That was the idea, but the Lord had another plan. We didn't even make it to the beach. As we drove toward the ocean I was compelled to ask my friend, "Could you please turn the car around? We need to go back to your house. I need to speak to your roommate. I need to witness to her." It was very clear that I had to do that. My friend didn't understand exactly what I was saying, but she could tell it was important.

Back at the house Emily was lying in bed feeling very ill. She said it must be the flu, but it seemed to all of us that it was something more serious. I asked her if she wanted me to take her to the hospital or call a doctor. She said she probably needed to see a doctor, but first she wanted to pray. I asked her, "Can we pray together?" She said that would be okay.

In Emily's bedroom there were pictures of Indian gurus all around, and on her shelves were various ritual objects and books. I also knew that her roommate, my friend, was devoted to the Hindu god Krishna. She was part of the international Hari Krishna movement. I said to Emily, "I will pray with you now, but we will pray only to Jesus Christ and to Our Lady who will intercede with Him for you. That's who I will be praying to and no one else." Emily said that would be fine. I asked Emily if she had been baptized, and she said yes, Episcopalian. With her permission, I began with a consecration prayer of St. Louis Mary de Montfort, in which baptism vows are renewed.

> I, a faithless sinner, renew and ratify today in thy hands, O Immaculate Mother, the vows of my Baptism. I renounce forever Satan, his pomps and works, and I give myself entirely to Jesus Christ, the Incarnate Wisdom, to carry my cross after Him all the days of my life, and to be more faithful to Him than I have ever been before. In the presence of all the heavenly court, I choose thee this day for my Mother and Mistress. I deliver and consecrate to thee, as thy slave, my body and soul, my goods, both interior and exterior, and even the value of all my good actions, past, present and future, leaving to thee the entire and full right of disposing of me, and all that belongs to me, without exception, according to thy good pleasure, for the greater glory of God, in time and eternity. Amen.

After our prayers I called a doctor to make an appointment, and Emily went to see him that afternoon. When I came back to visit her the next day, I asked if she would be willing to go to a Catholic Church and have a priest perform the sacrament of the anointing of the sick. I really didn't know exactly what I was proposing. I had just finished taking RCIA (Rite of Christian Initiation for Adults) classes but still didn't understand that a non-Catholic couldn't receive the sacraments. I also wasn't sure about the details of anointing the sick, but it sounded like the right thing to do. After all she was sick!

Emily said it was okay, so I called the local Catholic Church and talked to a very nice priest there, Father Joseph. He was very gracious.

I said to him, "I am with a woman who is sick. Could you pray over her?" Here I was, a stranger calling out of the blue trying to help a woman I hardly knew who was not even Christian with an unknown illness. It's obvious that I didn't understand what the situation required, but Father Joseph could hear my total belief in the power of prayer and the sacraments and the priesthood. Without hesitating he said, "Of course. Bring her over." Emily agreed to go.

We went together over to this small, local church in Makawao, St. Joseph's Church, and there we met Father Joseph. He asked Emily what her background was. She explained that she had been raised high Episcopalian, but for the past thirty years had been living in Maui practicing New Age and Hinduism. God's grace was with Father Joseph. This wonderful priest talked to her for the longest time and prayed with her and blessed her. When we left, Emily felt much better, and seemed to appreciate what had happened.

During the next two weeks, Malia and I visited Emily every day. My old friend would leave us alone, and the three of us would do the rosary together and talk and pray. When our vacation was over, Emily made a special effort to accompany us to the airport and bid us farewell. As we were leaving she surprised us with the gift of a Hawaiian flower lei, which she had custom-made exactly like a rosary. That was our goodbye present. It was so beautiful.

After we left, Emily joined the RCIA program at St. Joseph's — the same church with the same priest we had met during our visit. We kept in touch with Emily by phone. Her health was improving and she seemed very happy. God was guiding her to truth and fullness of faith.

A year and a half later Malia and I returned to Maui. RCIA at St. Joseph's took about two years, and in only a few months' time Emily was to be initiated into the Church at the Easter Vigil. We were distressed to hear, however, that Emily was almost ready to quit the program. The sponsor that the church had assigned to her for her second year had been a disappointment. The two women did not have good rapport, and the sponsor only attended about half of the RCIA classes and events. Emily felt quite abandoned, as though she had no support in building up her faith. It's very important that catechumens like Emily have a good sponsor, someone that really cares and helps and teaches. Since I have been a practicing Catholic I have served half a dozen times as an RCIA sponsor, and I've learned how important it is to be present. Sponsors need to be models of the Christian life.

Emily's sponsor didn't meet with her or pray with her or even go to Mass consistently. Emily had not formed a circle of Christian friends yet, and she could feel the pressure of her New Age friends, who were urging her to wise up and return to her former way of life. She had been living on an island for thirty years with only New Age friends, so you can imagine how hard that would be to cope with. So Emily was at a loss. She begged Malia and I to move to Maui just for a short while and be there for her, to sponsor her for these last few months and go to RCIA and church with her, to pray with her. She really needed direct help, but unfortunately, we couldn't provide it. Malia was in the middle of her school year and it was important that she complete it. We prayed hard.

On the last Sunday of our vacation, one day before our return to California, Malia, Emily and I decided to go to Mass on the other side of the island at Saint Therese's Church in Kihei. We arrived in time for the ten o'clock Mass. I knew we needed the communion of saints and the help of God like never before. I said to my daughter, "Malia, let's offer up our communion for our friend Emily, for her need to find a sponsor who will care about her like we do, who will be present for her, who will physically support her and spiritually support her by praying for her and praying with her." And I said, "You and I believe in the communion of saints. We know without a doubt that they hear us and are ready to help."

At that point we did not know much about Saint Therese of Lisieux. We knew vaguely that she was Mother Teresa's saint, and we knew that she had wanted to be a missionary. We didn't know her personally yet, but by the end of this day, we certainly would. During communion we begged her to please intercede for us. After Mass we prayed for a while in the adoration chapel, then we went outside to say the rosary at the Saint Therese statue in the garden.

Malia and I did not tell Emily that during Mass we had offered up our communion for her, or that we had asked Saint

Therese for help during our adoration time, but when we sat down to pray the rosary outside, I pulled out the only holy card I had with me. It was a card of Saint Therese and it showed her novena prayer:

Saint Therese, Little Flower,
please pick me a rose from the heavenly garden,
and send it to me with a message of love.
Ask God to grant me the favor I thee implore,
and tell Him I will love Him more and more.
Amen.

So that's all I had, that one little holy card. I didn't know anything at the time about novenas: that they take nine days, that they require a certain prayer formula and all of that. We just prayed very hard, combining the rosary with the novena prayer and really, really having faith in the intercession of St. Therese and Our Lady.

I guess we were there about two hours — Mass, adoration, the rosary — altogether it was about two hours of prayer. And then we decided to go to the beach, go snorkeling and give it up to God. We handed it over to God, put it all in His hands, and the three of us drove off to enjoy a sunny, fun afternoon at the beach.

Around six o'clock that evening we packed up and headed back to Emily's house on the other side of Maui. We were all hungry, so we stopped at a Thai restaurant along the way, very close to St. Therese's church. As we were deciding what to order, I noticed a familiar-looking woman across the dining room having dinner alone. Many years earlier I had lived in Kona, on the big island, where I knew a woman named Anne. In the middle of my magazine career, she had tried to evangelize me. She was a gospel-quoting Southern Baptist with a Bible tucked under her arm and a world of persistence. Although I thought she was a nice enough person and well-meaning, I had dismissed her at the time without much thought. So here we are twenty-two years later, sitting in this restaurant, and I say to Malia, "Go ask that woman if her name is Anne. See if she wants to join us."

Malia goes over to her and asks, "Is your name Anne? My mother would like to know. It is? Well, we would you like to come and sit with us."

Sure enough it was her, and she accepted Malia's invitation. As she approached our table, more recollections of twenty-two years ago came to mind. "Uh-oh." I thought. "That woman tried so hard to evangelize me. She was someone who would not be denied. All Emily needs right now is to hear a bunch of anti-Catholic talk."

My fears made me a little nervous at first, a little rude. Anne, on the other hand, was very kind, very caring. When she asked what had brought us to Maui I went ahead and told her. "We are here on vacation, but mostly we're here to support our good friend Emily. After thirty years of following New Age here on this island she is becoming a Catholic. She's having some difficulties, and we're trying to help her."

Anne gave me a rather startled look and said, "You don't know this, but over the past twenty years, I have become a Catholic. I sponsor people in the RCIA program. I am the answer to your prayer."

I said, "What prayer?" I said. "What do you know about our prayer?"

"Today at three o'clock, while I was at home praying, I felt moved to come over to this side of the island and go to Mass at Saint Therese's. It's not even my church. I just got out of five o'clock Mass. After Mass I came straight to this restaurant to have dinner."

Anne knew that she had been waiting for someone. She knew the Lord was calling her to go to that church and that restaurant, and when three strangers asked her to have dinner with them, she wasn't surprised. She went on to say that St. Therese, the Carmelite nun, was her saint, and that she herself was a third-order Carmelite. Talk about the communion of saints! Emily told Anne her story, and without hesitation, Anne said she would change her Easter vacation plans. Rather than go back to Arkansas to visit her family (who were still Baptist) she would stay on Maui and serve as Emily's sponsor and be her support system. She would take her by the hand and walk her all the way through the Easter Vigil.

It was a perfect match. Anne was a single woman in her fifties, the same as Emily, and she lived half way up a mountain on the other side of the island. The women lived two houses away from one another! They even attended the same church, but had never met. You could not have put Emily's profile into a computer and found a better sponsor. Thank you, St. Therese Little Flower, for your miraculous intercession.

So saints do work. I want to make that clear: Saints hear us and are glad to be called upon to intercede. It's a beautiful thing. It's a beautiful gift of God. It's His grace at work in the world.

Chapter Three
Preach Without Preaching

Dr. Bill Schaefer had been our family physician for almost fifteen years. He was raised Episcopalian, but for as long as I had known him he was a practicing Tibetan Buddhist. I was a New Ager for nearly all of those years, and found his religious views one more good reason for our family to go to him. After my conversion I began to include Dr. Schaefer in my prayers. I don't recall that I evangelized him energetically, but he was aware that my Christian faith had become the center of my life. I gave him a Miraculous Medal, which I know he kept with him, and I also gave him a green scapular, a sacramental through which Our Lady moves people to conversion.

Whenever I prayed the "Preach Without Preaching" prayer written by Cardinal Newman, which was very dear to Mother Teresa, I always thought of Dr. Schaefer.

> Dear Jesus,
> Help us to spread your fragrance everywhere we go.
> Flood our souls with your spirit and life.
> Penetrate and possess our whole being so utterly
> that our lives may only be a radiance of yours.
> Shine through us, and be so in us,
> that every soul we come in contact with
> may feel your presence in our soul.
> Let them look up and see no longer us but only Jesus.

Stay with us, and then we shall begin to shine as you
    shine;
so to shine as to be a light to others;
the light, O Jesus, will be all from you,
none of it will be ours; it will be you,
shining on others through us.
Let us thus praise you in the way you love best:
By shining on those around us.
Let us preach you without preaching,
not by words but by our example,
by the catching force, the sympathetic influence
of what we do,
the evident fullness of the love our hearts bear to you.
Amen.

Malia and I had no idea how our prayers were affecting the soul of our family doctor. Then one day, as he greeted me in his office, he announced, "That mother of yours keeps calling me."

I thought he meant my mother in Seattle, who had called him many times as she was undergoing chemotherapy. Dr. Schaefer helped direct a cancer clinic in Tijuana and my mother trusted him. They knew each other well enough to be in regular contact.

So I said to Dr. Schaefer, "What does she want?"

He answered, "I don't know!"

"Well, what did she say on the phone?"

"I don't mean Katherine. I mean that other mother. The one you keep talking about. The one on that medal you gave me."

"What do you mean?"

"Three times now," he said, "Mary has appeared to me in dreams. She always looks exactly the same. There is no doubt in my mind that it is her." He explained that she didn't speak. She would step toward him, and by this motion she was, as he said, "calling him."

My daughter and I were curious to know exactly what this dream figure looked like, so we asked the doctor, who was also a talented artist, to draw a picture of her. A few weeks later, Dr. Schaefer gave us a beautiful color sketch of the image. He had drawn it himself. It was Our Lady of Guadalupe. Dr. Schaefer worked in Mexico and spoke Spanish fluently so he was very involved in the culture and the language. Perhaps I shouldn't have been surprised to see Blessed Mother appear to him in this way. He asked me, "What do you think she wants?"

"What do you want when you give people your business card?" I answered. "You want them to come to your clinic. You're a doctor. You want them to come and get well. I'm sure she wants you to come to her house."

Dr. Schaefer laughed. "Where does she live?"

"In the church, of course. Why don't you come with us?"

Dr. Schaefer said okay.

I thought the best place to take a middle-aged, Tibetan Buddhist O.M.D. [Doctor of Oriental Medicine] who had never seen the inside of a Catholic Church would be to a healing Mass. What a great place to take a doctor! So I brought him along with me to Father Jerry Bevilacqua's charismatic

Mass and healing service in San Diego. He was overwhelmed by the experience. He even began telling patients about theses services, and referred a few to Father Jerry.

Dr. Schaefer began attending Mass with us as often as he could. That wasn't so often at first, mainly, I think, because of his responsibilities in Mexico. But Our Lady never gave up on him. She kept sending him patients wearing Miraculous Medals around their neck. She even sent the wife of a former Catholic priest to him, who was dying of cancer. He and the former priest spent time together talking about the ins and outs of the faith.

One day Dr. Schaefer called me and asked if I would like to visit a cancer clinic that had just opened in Tijuana. He was really proud of this new facility, which he had helped organize, and he wanted to give me a tour. I was now a member of Mother Teresa's Lay Missionaries of Charity. The Missionaries of Charity have a seminary and orphanages in Tijuana, and I told Dr. Schaefer that the next time I went to deliver clothing to one on the orphanages, I would stop by the clinic and see him.

About this same time, the Blue Army of Our Lady of Fatima came to San Diego and offered Masses and rosaries in the presence of their statue of Blessed Mother, which is a replica of the original in Portugal. The Blue Army had come to San Diego the year before, and at that time I had left a rosary with the statue's caretaker. He had said he would carry the rosary with the statue during its travels. Many people do this as a sign of devotion. After one of the Lady of Fatima

Masses, I approached the caretaker again and asked if he remembered the rosary I had left with him during his previous visit. I was hoping I might retrieve it. Of course he didn't, but he was very understanding. I described it to him, and he said that he would look for it. I didn't realize that no one asks for their rosary to be returned. So he was surprised, but very accommodating.

The caretaker left the church for a little while, and when he returned he had in his hand a beautiful gold rosary. He said that he was unable to distinguish exactly which rosary I had given him among the many he traveled with. But this one, he explained, was special, and he wanted me to have it. "When this rosary was given to us, it was silver. In the time it has been with us, it has turned to gold. That's what happens sometimes. I don't try to explain it. I usually give these rosaries to the sick and dying, but you may have it."

I accepted the caretaker's gift and left praying about what he had told me. I thought, "I'm not sick or dying, am I?"

Two weeks later I woke up knowing that I was finally going to visit Dr. Schaefer in Tijuana. I called him up and asked, "Can I go visit your clinic today?"

He said it was not the best day for him. He had an extra heavy patient load. It was not a good day for me to go to Tijuana either. I had house guests arriving at the airport to pick up, and it was pouring rain. But none of that could get in the way of my going to Tijuana. When I'm called, I go, and I knew there was a call. This was the day, regardless of any inconveniences.

Dr. Schaefer could tell how adamant I was. He agreed to let me visit, but warned me that he might have little or no time to show me around. That was good enough for me. I drove to Tijuana and found the clinic, and while the doctor made his daily rounds I sat in the waiting room. As I waited, I prayed the rosary using the beads given to me by the caretaker from the Blue Army. As I prayed, a woman approached me. I recognized her as someone from San Diego, a woman named Sharon, who had been my neighbor many years earlier. In those days we had both been New Agers. We hadn't seen each other for years, and she didn't know anything about my conversion.

Sharon greeted me and asked if I had cancer. Why was I here? Was I sick, too? I told her no, that I was waiting for Dr. Schaefer and hoping to get a tour of the clinic.

Then she asked, "What's that in your hands?"

I told her it was a rosary. And she said, "Oh! Well, do you think you could come and pray the rosary in my father's room? He used to go to church with my mother before she died. That was twelve years ago. He asked me, just recently, to go find her old rosary and bring it to him."

She had been unable to find it, but she knew how much it would mean to him if we could pray the rosary together. Sharon hadn't been to a Catholic Church since she was a child, had been in the New Age for the past thirty years, and couldn't remember the prayers. I said, "Yes, of course. I'll be happy to."

Sharon had to leave for an appointment, but she left me

with her daughter and father in his private room. When we were nearly finished with the fourth decade of the rosary, there was a knock at the door. Dr. Schaefer and two colleagues were making rounds. They entered the room and watched us without interrupting. Then, during a pause, one of the doctors took the opportunity to call me out of the room. I was afraid I might be in trouble.

The doctor asked me, "What were you doing in that room?"

I showed him the rosary and said, "We were praying the rosary in honor of the Mother of God."

The doctor looked at the beads and looked at me and said, "Go back in the room and keep doing whatever you are doing. We told this patient earlier today to go home, that it was time for him to get his things in order and prepare for his funeral. He has only a few days left. An hour ago he was terribly upset, really in despair. Now he seems to be calm and peaceful. Whoever you are praying to, it is working. Keep it up."

That, almost word for word, is what this cancer specialist said to me. At least five people were witnessed to that day by the rosary from the Blue Army: Dr. Schaefer the Buddhist, his colleague who was a Jehovah's Witness, my New Age friend Sharon and her daughter, and Sharon's father.

Before I left, I gave the rosary to Sharon's father, and he asked if I would help his daughter to contact a priest and arrange for a Catholic funeral. This I did right away. Upon my return to San Diego, I called the monsignor at St. Mark's

Church, and for the next two weeks the priest or a deacon came to him every day with holy communion. He took confession. The priest ministered to his family, and to many of the friends and relatives (many of them fallen away Catholics) who visited him during his final days.

Dr. Schaefer and I attended the funeral, which was held in a Catholic Church. Afterwards he said to me, "I know this was no accident. What should I do now?"

I told him, "You sign up for RCIA." And so he did. It took him two years and two different parishes to complete RCIA because of his busy schedule, working two practices at two clinics. He finally made it to Easter Vigil at the age of forty-eight.

Our Lord knows when we are to be born and when we are to die. He knew that Dr. Schaefer only had a little time left. Over the next few years, the Lord used him to witness beautifully to the love of God and Our Lady. When he learned that he had cancer, the end came suddenly.

As it approached, we tried desperately to reach Father Jerry Bevilacqua, who had drawn him to faith years before. Father Jerry was out of town, but he came as soon as he was able, and saw Dr. Schaefer in his hospital bed before he died. We're so grateful. He started out with Father Jerry and he ended up with Father Jerry in his last hours. Thank God, Dr. Schaefer is with Our Lady in the family of God.

Chapter Four
Jesus is Lord

Rosemarie was one of my teachers in the Course in Miracles. In the heyday of the New Age she was well known, not only for her Course in Miracles seminars, which were very popular, but also for her music. She was a songwriter and performer, and did concerts all over the country. Her recordings were available everywhere. When my conversion began, Rosemarie and I lost touch with each other, and then she moved from Southern California to Washington. Like most of my old friends in the New Age, she had no idea what was happening in my life.

One sunny San Diego day the phone rang and it was Rosemarie. She knew that I had a comfortable guest room, that I lived near the beach, and that she had always been welcome in my home. She was passing through San Diego and wondered if she could stay with me. She had watched Malia grow up, and was looking forward to seeing her as well.

Rosemarie was surprised by my hesitation. "You know, Rosemarie, since I last saw you I've gone back to the Catholic Church. I'm not sure it's a good idea for you to stay here. What are you into now?"

"I still do the Course in Miracles. But now I'm also into alchemical hypnotherapy and the I Ching. The I Ching is amazing."

I wanted nothing to do with any of this stuff. "Well, Rosemarie, let me pray about this. I will get back to you. Why don't you call me tomorrow."

The next afternoon Rosemarie called me from a pay phone near the freeway. "Moira, I'm headed back north. May I stay at your place tonight? Just for one night?"

I had prayed on it. It seemed to be okay to say yes, so I did. "But leave all your I Ching stuff in the car." I said. "I don't want any of your New Age objects in my house."

I thought, "Well, that will offend her." But it didn't. She still wanted to come.

So I made it doubly clear, "Just bring in your nightgown and your toothbrush. Everything else stays in the car."

When Rosemarie arrived the conversation was awkward at first. I told her a little bit about my conversion and the peace I now felt. Rosemarie was respectful, but didn't have much to say on the topic. I think she was a little irritated. As dinner time approached, I suggested that she and Malia and I go out for Chinese food. That seemed like a good idea for a guest who was practicing the I Ching. I was glad when she accepted the invitation; I was still not quite comfortable having her in my house.

Dinner seemed to energize Rosemarie, and through most of the meal she focused the conversation on New Age brainwashing. It reminded me of my past life. I was so disturbed that I started praying right there in the restaurant. All through the meal — as we talked, as we ordered our food, as we ate — I prayed silently.

The Holy Spirit was at work. As I prayed I recalled that ten years earlier, when I was at her house for a Course in Miracles workshop, Rosemarie had brought in a bouquet of gorgeous red roses. She was beaming with joy about these roses and about the nursery where she had bought them. She told us that the shop had a beautiful sign out front that said, "Jesus is Lord." The sign, she said, had delighted her, and her joy was overflowing. I remember thinking at the time what a strange thing that was: that a New Age teacher would be so excited by a sign proclaiming Jesus as Lord.

Recalling this event gave me hope. I was especially hopeful because just a few days before I had been to a healing Mass with Father Jerry Bevilacqua. In his homily, Father Jerry cited the words of St. Paul: "No one can say 'Jesus is Lord' except by the Holy Spirit." [I Corinthians 12, 3] Those words had stuck in my mind ever since. I thought to myself, "If Rosemarie could declare to a New Age class, with such joy, that Jesus is Lord, it must have been by the Holy Spirit. If she could say it then, maybe she could say it again. Maybe the Holy Spirit could move her to say it with faith."

So I got very bold and I invited Rosemarie to go with us to a Taize service. Taize is a beautiful Christian liturgy with its own unique chants and prayers, and a long, very moving period of veneration of the cross. The Taize tradition began in France during the past century and has become a powerful movement across Europe, across denominations. I told Rosemarie a little about Taize and explained that a service would be held that evening at our church. "If you are curious, we can go there directly from the restaurant. It's not just for Catholics. It would be a wonderful place for you to pray and meditate."

Rosemarie said she would like to see what it was all about, so we paid the check and headed to the church. We were right on time, the service began, and I felt certain that Rosemarie, being a singer, would at least be fascinated by the chants. That turned out not to be the case. She did not like it at all. She was very confused by and resistant to everything that was happening. After less than ten minutes she insisted on leaving. I explained to her that, for my own part, I needed to stay. "To me, it's very relaxing, very meditative, very contemplative, and I can't leave just yet. In other words, I've got the car keys and you're stuck."

Malia had an inspiration. "Why don't you and I go to the adoration chapel. It's a beautiful space. You can bring a book. We'll wait for Mom there."

Off they went and made themselves at home in the chapel. Rosemarie, of course, didn't know anything about the blessed sacrament, the candles, the sacred images. She also didn't know about the need for silence. She started asking Malia lots of questions. "What is this place? What is that gold thing up there on the altar? Who is the man in the picture holding the baby? What do people do here?"

Malia patiently answered her questions, one by one. She told Rosemarie about the monstrance and the host and the presence of Jesus. "He's actually here, you know. It looks like bread, but it's really Jesus. He's there, He's really present. Just start talking to him."

Out of the mouths of babes, as the Gospel tells us. "Start praying to him, start talking to him." And that's what Rosemarie did. She happened to find on one of the tables a copy of *Miracle Hour*, by the Catholic charismatic Linda Schubert. She picked up this wonderful little book and started doing some of the prayers given there.

> Loving Father, I choose to forgive everyone in my life, including myself, because You have forgiven me. Thank You, Lord, for this grace. I forgive myself for all my sins, faults and failings. I forgive myself for not being perfect. I accept myself and make a decision to stop picking on myself and being my own worst enemy. I release the things held against myself, free myself from bondage and make peace with myself today, by the power of the Holy Spirit.
>
> I forgive my MOTHER for any negativity and unlove she may have extended to me throughout my life, knowingly or unknowingly. For any abuse of any sort I do forgive her today. For any way that she did not provide a deep, full, satisfying mother's blessing I do forgive her today. I release her from bondage and make peace with her today.
>
> I forgive my FATHER for any negativity and unlove he may have extended to me throughout my life, knowingly or unknowingly. For any and all abuses, unkind acts, hurts, and deprivations I do forgive him today. For any way that I did not receive a full, satisfying father's

blessing I forgive him today. I release him from bondage and make peace with him today.

I forgive my SPOUSE for any negativity and unlove extended throughout our time together. For all the wounds of our relationship I do forgive my spouse today. I release my spouse from bondage and make peace between us today. . . .

The Taize service ended at ten o'clock. I was feeling tired and ready to go home, but when I entered the adoration chapel I saw that Rosemarie was not ready to leave. She and Malia and I stayed there praying until after midnight. When we finally left, as we were walking to my car in the parking lot, Rosemarie turned to me and said, "I know it now: Jesus is Lord." Exactly the words she had reacted to so strongly a decade before! We all laughed with joy when she said that. It was really great. And she said it with such conviction that we knew the Holy Spirit had touched her.

Rosemarie stayed in our home for three more days. When she left, she was headed for Oregon, where she was scheduled to speak and perform her music at a major Course in Miracles conference. A few days later she called us and said that when she got on stage she couldn't sing. Instead she talked to the audience about Jesus, and lead prayers to Jesus and the Holy Spirit. People got restless and the organizers of the conference were very upset. Although she found out later that some in the audience were inspired to conversion by her words, she was asked to leave.

"What do I do now?" she asked.

"Father Jerry Bevilacqua is coming to Seattle this weekend for a retreat and a healing Mass. You need to see him"

Rosemarie agreed to go, taking her sister, who was also involved in the New Age, with her. Father Jerry is an Augustinian priest with a gift of healing through the Holy Spirit. During the service, as he was standing at the front of the church, Father Jerry said, "Someone here has Lyme disease."

Rosemarie thought he must be talking about someone else, but when he repeated his words and no one responded, she stood up, very nervous, and said, "I have Lyme disease."

I was not aware of it at the time, but Rosemarie's health was declining. Lyme disease was beginning to affect her joints. Her blood and organs were beginning to show signs that indicated her condition could become life-threatening.

Father Jerry immediately came over to her. He told her about her symptoms, describing exactly her prognosis the same as her medical doctors had described. Then he said, "Jesus wants to heal you. He is healing you now." Then he prayed over her for about twenty minutes. When he was finished he said, "You are healed. It will take about a week for all the signs of this disease to leave your body but, after that, go to a doctor and get it checked out."

About two weeks later, Rosemarie went to her doctor, who confirmed that she was healed. It was nothing less than a miracle, and as Father Jerry told her later in private, not only was she cured physically, but also spiritually. Over the months that followed he met with her in person and by phone, and eventually Rosemarie and her sister entered the RCIA program at a Catholic church in Washington. She and her sister are now charismatic Christian women of deep faith. "Jesus is Lord." Thank you, Holy Spirit.

Chapter Five
Forgive Us Our Trespasses

When I first moved to the San Diego area in the early 1980s I knew almost no one here. Shortly after my arrival, however, I met Carol in a prenatal class. Like myself, Carol was about to have her first child. She had recently relocated from the Pacific Northwest and had graduated from the University of Washington the same year as I. She lived in my neighborhood, and it was inevitable that we would become friends. Over the next few years, Carol and I became almost like sisters, as did our daughters, Malia and Leslie. She shared my interest in New Age, although her involvement was less serious.

It was right around Malia's tenth birthday when I learned that Carol and her husband, Mark, were getting divorced. She and Leslie were moving back to the Northwest. This was a shock to us, especially when we learned the cause: Carol's husband, a respected and successful business executive, had admitted to physically abusing their daughter. It was one of the most humiliating and painful things I have ever witnessed. After Carol and Leslie left, Malia and I missed them terribly, and we felt a lot of rage toward Mark. He continued to live in the house near us, and we saw him fairly regularly in the neighborhood. I think it's true that never in my life have I felt such anger – it might have been hatred — toward any other person. It was a burden I carried with me that, out of consideration for everyone involved, had to remain a secret. I never expected it to heal.

Shortly after my recommitment to the Church, I began to attend RCIA classes. Even though I had completed all my sacraments, I was in many ways like a catechumen. I needed a total reeducation. In one of these classes, a visiting priest analyzed the Our Father for us with great care. This priest made it absolutely, black and white clear to me the truth of the verse, "Forgive us our trespasses as we forgive those who trespass against us." There was no exception, no compromise, he said, to the rule that as Christians we are called to forgive; that it is only in forgiving that we ourselves will be forgiven. When I heard this explained so straightforwardly, I realized, "Jesus is talking to me."

I remember sitting in the classroom thinking, "I am only human. It's not easy for me to forgive. Especially someone like Mark" — that's exactly who I was thinking of — "who has completely betrayed my friends and ruined their lives. It's so hard!"

So I said a prayer. "Lord, I am only human and you are divine. Please take my human heart with its finite ability to truly forgive and consecrate it to your own compassionate, merciful heart. Place your heart, Lord Jesus, on mine, and give me the strength to forgive this man."

It took time for this prayer to bear fruit. First I began to actually let my eyes meet Mark's when I would see him in public. Then I sent him a Christmas card. During the year that followed Carol called from the Northwest and asked if I would mind contacting Mark to make sure he sent some furniture and other belongings up to her. She didn't know who else she could ask. That was a big test for me, but I was able to call him up and go visit him without communicating the anger I felt toward him.

As we went through his garage, sorting out the stuff that needed to be shipped north, I could feel the great shame and humiliation that Mark had been carrying with him. We never addressed the issue directly, but I was inspired by the words of the prayer, "preach without preaching." By treating him with compassion and respect, I hoped that healing might follow — in both of us.

One afternoon I needed to go see Mark again — this was probably the fourth or fifth time — and Malia and I decided that she would go with me. When the two of us arrived together, Mark was very surprised. He probably thought that no matter how much consideration I might show him, I would certainly keep my own daughter at a distance. He was visibly moved.

Malia and I went back out to the garage and were moving things around, checking our lists, when Mark came out to talk to us. We were standing there with the garage door wide open, boxes all around. Mark stood there looking at us both and said, "How can the two of you ever forgive me? I am so terribly sorry."

I had imagined that moment for months and my answer

came readily. "Mark, believe me, we cannot forgive you on our own. But, through God's grace, we have been given hearts of compassion for you. May God bless you and forgive you."

He looked at us with an expression of sadness and relief, and said, "Thank you. Thank you for saying that. Thank you to your God."

A few days later we finished our work at Mark's house. As I was saying good-bye to him, he said to me, "Moira, I think I want to know more about God."

He said it with sincerity. He really meant it. He wanted to know the God that would put such compassion in our hearts for him. I invited him to church.

Mark began to come to Mass with us regularly, one or two times a month. We could tell that the homilies and readings spoke to him deeply, and I wasn't surprised when about a year later he asked if I would sponsor him in RCIA.

"Of course I will," I said.

Once Mark made his decision, some unanticipated difficulties arose. There was a lot of spiritual warfare. In the three months leading up to his first RCIA class, Mark stopped going to church for a while, always finding some excuse. His behavior was very confusing to me, and when I asked him if he had changed his mind, he became angry. He stopped answering the phone when I called and avoided me in public. I told the priest, "Mark and I aren't even speaking. How on Earth are we going to manage to go to RCIA?"

One day late in August, just a few days before the first

RCIA session, I went alone to the adoration chapel and just surrendered myself to the Lord. "Lord, I know you've called this man. I know you're asking me to help bring his soul to your truth. How do you want me to do it? I certainly don't know the way."

After my prayer I went to morning Mass, offered up the Eucharist for Mark, then went home and prayed and fasted all day. After almost eight hours, I finally got a message from the Lord. I heard it in my mind unmistakably, "Call and make an appointment."

Of course! He's a businessman. I called Mark at his office and asked him if he had his datebook. "Can we make an appointment?"

He said, "I think so."

I made an appointment with him: ten minutes to seven in the evening in the church parking lot, next Tuesday night.

"What's this for?" he asked.

"Well, there's going to be an introductory presentation about the Catholic Church." I didn't say anything about RCIA or our recent conflicts.

He answered, "I'll see you there."

That was the beginning, and it ended up being a fabulous program, a beautiful time. The Lord truly gave me the grace to help escort this soul home to God's house, to put aside all bitterness, anger, resentment and division, so that we could sit side by side every week, in RCIA and in church. Since then there has been a huge healing in Mark's family. He and Carol have been able to reconcile to the point where he is now part of his daughter's life. He has gone to visit them and spend time with them, and at birthdays and graduations and other important days, he is now there for his daughter. It's just a beautiful healing story. The Lord gave Mark the grace to reconcile and make retribution for his offenses while he's still here on Earth, and to offer a father's love to his child that they thought was lost forever.

Part Three

New Age Notebook

Ghosts and Demons

Nowhere in Church teachings does it say that souls of the dead wander the Earth, appearing to us and influencing our lives in the form of ghosts. Still, it was my experience for many years as a clairvoyant, as a healer, and as a practitioner of occult sciences that I was getting information and powers from spiritual entities. I saw them and heard them and felt them. I saw their actions in the world. I wasn't calling on the Holy Spirit, or on Jesus and Mary. It wasn't them or their allies. And so I look to scripture and I look to the Catechism to understand who these beings are. These sources teach that they are demons. Jesus and the prophets and the saints did battle with these spiritual forces, and that's why I refer to them as they did: as demons, evil spirits, fallen angels, the Evil One, Satan, the Devil. These are the terms we have inherited to refer to the spiritual beings that drive a wedge between ourselves and God.

Greater Works

New Agers love to misquote the Bible, especially alternative healers. Jesus says in John, chapter 14, "Amen, amen, I say to you, whoever believes in me will do the works that I do, and will do greater ones than these."

New Agers stop right there. They say, "We can do greater works, just as Jesus predicted."

These people don't quote what follows: "Because I am going to the Father, and whatever you ask in my name I will do, so that the Father may be glorified in the Son. If you ask anything of me in my name I will do it."

This part psychic healers leave out. But do not be confused. Unless they are working in the name of Jesus, and unless they are glorifying God the Father, then they're not following the words of Jesus. They are not working with the Holy Spirit.

The gifts of the Holy Spirit are works of service so that the body of Christ may be built up. They are not used as a display of power. They do not aggrandize the individual.

New Thought Churches

Mary Baker Eddy started Christian Science Churches and, from there, Ernest Holmes started teaching Religious Science, and from there the modern Unity Church and Unitarian Universalists came into being. A lot of people don't realize that these are not Christian churches. They teach the Holy Trinity of Me, Myself and I. The words that they use for God are "life spirit," "universal mind," "supreme intelligence," "the great architect." Basically, their God is a consciousness. There is no savior.

If you go back to the original writings of the founders of these churches, Mary Baker Eddy and Ernest Holmes, you'll see that they call their teaching "New Thought." This is what I was trained in for many years. New Thought is about changing your consciousness. It's really not even a religion; it's a psychology of brainwashing.

They teach that we are part of an infinite mind. God is an infinite formless energy, a cosmic force. We give it form, shaping it into a world through our thoughts. We are the absolute creators of our world. If we change our thinking, then we change the conditions of our life. We can manifest, because our pure will is the law of our universe. New Thought supports this idea with Bible references and, in fact, teaches whole courses in the Bible using this "metaphysical" interpretation.

Hypnotherapy

On the back of my Catholic church bulletin I read, "Destress your life by the power of hypnotism."

I called the parish secretary to find out more about this ad, and she told me, "Yes. Monsignor knows that the ad is in there. He approves of it. He believes that hypnotherapy is a legitimate part of psychotherapy."

After that I called the hypnotist and she said, "Well, I'm not a Christian and I'm not a psychotherapist. I took a six-week course in hypnotism, and the Course in Miracles is my textbook."

Every red flag I could think of went up.

I am still a certified hypnotherapist, although I don't practice anymore. The problem with hypnosis has to do with will. Whenever someone hypnotizes you, whether it's in a nightclub or in a therapeutic setting, you surrender your will. That's where it's dangerous. The hypnotist could have been trained

138 ✝ RANSOMED FROM DARKNESS

at a Dianetics institute, for all you know. They might be trained in clear-mind training or autogenic training. So stay away from any kind of hypnotism unless you are certain of the background of the therapist. If you are dealing with chronic pain or addiction, look for a Christian psychologist.

Crystals

Any crystals that you've ever been given or purchased – quartz crystals, not lead crystal — you don't know whose hands they have passed through. They all have a history, and you don't know who has cut them or arranged them or handled them. Any crystal can be programmed. When it is programmed, a spirit is attached to it, and I don't mean the Holy Spirit. Demon spirits use crystals to enter your house. They are doorways.

New Agers know that the first thing they have to do is clear their crystals. They take them to the ocean and wash them in the sea to send evil spirits away. Christians could use blessed salt and holy water for the same purpose, but why bother? Throw them away. Get them out of the house.

A Caution About Deliverance

Deliverance is not something to undergo without preparation and knowledge. The best person to perform deliverance is a priest. A priest is protected through the sacrament of Holy Orders. By virtue of that sacrament he has been given the appropriate charism. There are also laypeople who have received from God the gift of delivering others from spirits through the power of the Holy Spirit. If you are in need of deliverance, you must find someone who you are sure has this gift.

The First Commandment

When you start dabbling in the New Age you break the First Commandment: "You shall not have other gods besides me." It is as simple as that. You are dabbling in idolatry. After that it gets easier to rationalize all the other Commandments and let them fall away. Your moral life goes out the window, and you make up your own rules, your own values. You become the author of your own life, with God no longer in charge.

Christian Attitude

In the New Age the emphasis is on the self — self idolatry, building up the self. The self does it all. The self can be enlightened, the self is the savior, the ego is in charge. A Christian attitude is different. It emphasizes nurturing the virtues of the soul, building humility, patience and service.

Martial Arts

The martial arts are part of the occult world. When you reach their upper levels, you learn meditations. When you practice these meditations, you're working with demon spirits. I'm not talking about little kids in elementary school who go down to the shopping center or the YMCA after school and take a class. I mean those who advance to higher levels. On the other hand, there is an association of Christian martial arts. There are churches that offer martial arts in a Christian way with Christian meditations for adults that want to advance.

Fast Enlightenment

In America we want everything fast. We want fast food and fast service and ATM machines, and all of that. We also want fast spirituality, fast enlightenment. All of this, of course, opposes the teachings of Jesus. For example, we know that Jesus redeemed us from sin by his resurrection, and then ascended into Heaven. Well, there are a number of outlets around the country selling fast ascension to anyone willing to pay for it.

Summit Lighthouse is one of these cults. It's actually worldwide. Their leader is Elizabeth Claire Prophet, who's even been on the cover of *The Wall Street Journal*. Prophet's followers call themselves "the Light Bearers of the World." Their guru, El Morya, is supposed to be an immortal ascended master. If you successfully complete their meditations and prayers, and follow their practices, you, too, will ascend. You don't even need to wait until you die. You can ascend right now in your ethereal body, and still be on Earth in your physical body doing the work of the immortal masters. Jesus himself, so they say, is one of them.

I know Summit Lighthouse uses prayers because I was involved with them. They use prayers and rosaries that are a complete mockery of the Catholic faith. Their rosaries have no cross, they have these sacred medals. The say the Our Father but they change the words. They say Hail Marys but they leave out the words "pray for us sinners . . ." They use the Prayer to St. Michael the Archangel for protection, but they call him "Lord Michael." He's an ascended master, too!

Heresies

It says in Deuteronomy, chapter 18: "When you come into the land which the Lord, our God, is giving you, you shall not learn to imitate the abominations of the people there. Let there not be found among you anyone who immolates his son or daughter in the fire — not a fortune-teller, soothsayer, charmer, diviner, or caster of spells, nor one who consults ghosts and spirits, or seeks oracles from the dead."

If we were to write this same list in modern terms, it would include the following:

Alchemical Hypnotherapy
Alchemy
Angel Guides
Angelic Channeling
Astral Cartography
Astral Projection
Astrology
Aura Work
Automatic Handwriting
Chakra Balancing
Channeling

Clairaudience

Clairsentience

Clairvoyance

Crystal Healing

Crystal Divination

Dousing

Eckankar

Energy Work

EST

Etheric Light Body Work

Firewalking

The Forum

Geomancy

Hands of Light

Hypnotism

The "I Am" Movement

I Ching

Laying of Stones

Medicine Wheel

Necromancy

New Thought

Numerology

Out-of-Body Work

Past-life Regression Therapy

Psychic Development

Psychic Healing

Rebirthing

Reiki
Shamanism
Silva Mind Control
Soul Travel
Spirit Guides
Spiritual Psychotherapy
Spiritualism
Table-Tipping
Tantra
Tarot Cards
Trance Mediums
Trance Work
Visualization
Wicca

This is what the Lord was referring to when he said "You are my chosen people. Do not fall prey to these things. Don't follow the gods of the pagans." Modern paganism goes by many names.

Discernment

One word that is absent from the New Age vocabulary is "discernment." It tells you in the Bible to test the spirits [1 John 4, 1-6], but New Agers rarely do. They'll say, "Let's go to this channeling. Let's go to this initiation. Let's go to this ritual." Every spirit falls into one category. Demons and angels are all the same.

In the Christian world, visionaries might have an apparition, or receive a locution. Then there is a rigorous system of discernment to determine whether these are true or false. One of the problems with the New Age is that people aren't under spiritual direction. There is no discernment process. A person might claim to be receiving messages from this spirit or this person or this saint when it's really the Evil One speaking.

Satan mocks all the gifts of the Holy Spirit. A Christian with deep humility and virtue who receives the gift of healing or knowledge or prophecy is completely different from a psychic who's not working in the name of Jesus. Psychic abilities mock the gifts of the Holy Spirit. If you're getting information from an entity in the psychic realm, a demon spirit is giving that information. I know this because I was a psychic.

The source of a message can be difficult to discern. For example, in Acts, chapter 16, Luke relates that a girl with an "oracular spirit" followed Paul, shouting, "These people are slaves of the most high God, who proclaim to you a way of salvation." Now this sounds like a good thing, but the girl's knowledge was not from God. It was demonic. After several days, Paul discerned this and said, "I command you in the name of Jesus Christ to come out of her."

So this was not the Holy Spirit, and Paul had to discern that. In the New Age they teach you a lot about how to develop these skills and work with these skills, but they don't ever tell you what spirits you're working with, and they don't tell you how to discern these spirits.

Prophecy

Paul tells us to "strive eagerly" for prophecy [1 Corinthians 14, 39]. Prophecy, a gift of the Holy Spirit, can be very effective in building up the Christian community. In the psychic world, however, prophecy is used to build up the self, to gain power over others, to impart power over others to clients.

Psychics use prophecy to invade boundaries. The Holy Spirit, on the other hand, has tremendous respect for persons. It's not going to let you learn the private secrets of others. Why would it? Does that bring encouragement and consolation? Does that strengthen the community? Does that promote salvation of the soul?

Pride and Humility

When you're working with spirit guides, demon spirits, they're going to give you miracles, they're going to give you signs and wonders. But these signs will be encouragement for pride. Remember, that was the first sin. Pride was the reason for the fall of Lucifer. Pride is the reason people want to become adept at gnosticism and other esoteric teachings. It's all based on pride. Why else would anyone strive to achieve that level of self-realization, of self-enlightenment, of self-fulfillment, of self-mastery, of self-centeredness?

Christ, on the other hand, asks us to surrender. So if you are wondering whether someone works with the Holy Spirit, look at their life. Do they have humility, or are they dominated by pride?

Eastern Meditation

A lot of people are involved in Eastern meditation practices. They are even taught at parishes, Christian retreat centers, and so forth. At one retreat center I saw a picture of a Buddhist monk who was coming to teach Christians how to meditate. His method is called Vipassana, or mindfulness meditation. This is a technique that empties your mind. (They didn't put this in the brochure.)

The Holy Spirit doesn't ask us to empty our minds. Paul tells us to take every thought captive [2 Corinthians 10, 5]. We're not supposed to use meditation to blank out our mind and enter a state of emptiness. We're supposed to put on the mind of Christ.

One God, Many Paths

People will ask, "Why is this religious system any different from Christianity? Aren't we all one? Isn't there one god? Aren't there many paths to the same goal?"

That's not what the Bible says. Moses told his people, "Don't follow pagan gods. Don't follow their ways. They do not follow our God." [Deuteronomy 18]

Some meditation systems — Hindu, Buddhist, New Age — teach you to become one with a god who is clearly different. This god is not called "good." He is a non-dualistic god, a god who claims that there is no such opposition as evil versus good. Evil and good are wrapped up together in one divine entity.

We're not taught that. That's not at all Christian teaching. We're taught that God is personal — not an impersonal energy force. We're taught that He's God the Father, that we actually can claim Him as our Father, that we are His sons and daughters and can inherit His kingdom [Matthew 23, 9]. We have salvation through him, and we're not lost children. So this is a very different god.

And we're not taught that the god of demons and the god of angels is the same god with one face. In Tibetan Buddhism, for example, spiritual warfare means that through meditation, you can, as a living person, meet angels and demons without fear. By your own efforts you can overcome your fear and achieve a level of enlightenment where good and evil are one. That's completely different from Christian spiritual warfare. That's not the spiritual warfare that Paul talks about in his letter to the Ephesians [6, 12]. We are waging a battle against principalities and powers of unseen worlds. These two religions are irreconcilable unless you distort their teachings.

Signs of the Spirits

When people are working with the Holy Spirit, the signs are humility, holiness, good morals. As John Paul II has written, "The spirit of Jesus received by the humble and docile heart of the believer brings about the flourishing of a Christian moral life and the witness of holiness." [*Splendor of Truth*, 108]

The sign of demons is corruption. They're liars. They lead a person deeper and deeper into sin. The invisible demons of the New Age movement usually lead a person into sexual sin. That one is pretty easy. They rationalize promiscuity.

They also bring with them a spirit of oppression, so that people feel oppressive guilt. The Holy Spirit shows us our sin, but it doesn't oppress us. It doesn't take us into a crushing state of despair. When the Holy Spirit convicts us of our sin it calls us to repentance, by which we are set free. That doesn't happen in the occult world. Demonic spirits draw a person deeper into sin.

Qigong

Some people, Christians included, believe that qigong will help deliver them from demons, because it teaches a certain kind of protective breath work. With this technique and certain meditations, they say that you can tap into a cosmic life force. With this life force you can construct a bubble of energy around yourself. You're connected to the sun, the stars, the moon, the earth, and everything else. You have that much power to call on, all the energy in the universe, and you can protect yourself with it. Does that match Christian teaching?

Yoga and the Body

Yoga in Sanskrit means "union," which in this context means quite specifically union with God. Yoga is not just some form of exercise like jogging or jazzercise or aerobics. The god of yoga is an impersonal deity who pervades the universe. So as a

Christian, yoga is not a program to enter into blindly.

In most yogic schools, the goal is to transcend the body through postures and breathing techniques, to use the body to detach yourself from the body. That's the whole point. And that has nothing to do with what the Bible tells us about the body. The Bible never says that our body is evil. That's gnosticism. We're told that our body is a temple of the Holy Spirit. [I Corinthians 3, 16; 6, 19] What is evil is sin. Sin may or may not involve our body.

We should be careful of any practice based on the belief that the body is inherently evil. In yoga, the spirit is held in bondage by the physical body, and the objective is to free one's self from that bondage. Having practiced it myself, I don't see how this can be reconciled with Christianity.

"Christ Consciousness"

New Agers usually don't talk about Jesus Christ. They say "cosmic Christ" or "Christ consciousness" or "Jesus, the ascended master." If you do certain practices, you're going to attain Christ consciousness. You're going to think like Christ and therefore you will actually be another Christ. *A Course in Miracles* says that we're all walking Christs. We just haven't awakened to that level of divinity in ourselves. When we do we will solve all the world's problems. There will be peace everywhere. No Holy Spirit needed. But if we are all working with our own private spirit guide, how do we make peace? I don't know. It sounds like certain chaos.

Divination

Divination is more than just fortune telling; it's also palm reading, crystal ball reading, water witching, dousing, tarot cards, tea leaf reading, numerology and the study of animal entrails, as in Santeria. There are also modern forms of divination which are presented as scientific. These include handwriting analysis, iridology (reading the eyes), and kinesiology, which a lot of holistic health healers use.

Divination gives people a feeling of control over their lives. But Satan, being the father of lies, deceives us through these instruments. Through these practices the human will weakens and Satan gets a foothold in our lives. The control that divination offers is the opposite of what the Bible teaches: that we have faith in God alone, that God is in control, that God is totally just and the Holy Spirit will guide us, through the Bible and the Church.

Part Four

Concerning A Course in Miracles

Chapter One
Genesis of the New Age Bible

When I first got involved in New Age in the mid-1970s, *A Course in Miracles* was something of a secret. A growing but small number of people knew about the book, which was only available through the organization that originally published it, the Foundation for Inner Peace. In the past three decades the fortunes of the work have changed dramatically. *A Course in Miracles* is now stocked in nearly every bookstore, and has been a continual bestseller. I call it the New Age bible. Others have called it "a third testament" of God to his people.

What I find most disturbing about *A Course in Miracles* is its acceptance by many in the Christian community. Christian booksellers carry it, and it can be found on the library shelves of churches, monasteries, seminaries and retreat centers, where it is even taught as a supplement to Christian teachings. Please be aware that *A Course in Miracles* is not Christian in any accepted sense of the word. As it openly declares, it is the dictated message of a spiritual entity who claims to reveal the true teachings of Jesus, whose message has been distorted by generations of misguided transcribers and corrupt interpreters. You may not be surprised to learn that, according to this entity, we are all equal to God.

A Course in Miracles is actually a set of three books: text, workbook and a manual for teachers. These books are also available in one paperback volume. The workbook is divided into 365 lessons, with the idea that the student will cover one lesson per day over a period of one year. These books are based on the experiences of Dr. Helen Schucman, a self-described atheist, who was a psychologist at Columbia University.

The story goes that Dr. Shucman and her colleague, Dr. William Thetford, had a difficult and antagonistic relationship, until one day they literally joined hands and vowed to help each other find a better way. After that, Dr. Schucman began to have psychic experiences. She had visions of ancient goddess worship. She also had a series of visions in which she saw "her book." One time she saw it wrapped in pearls, another time it was carried in a stork's pouch, yet another time it bore the name of the Greek god of healing, Asclepius.

Asclepius, according to pagan theology, was a son of Apollo, the Greek god of Wisdom, and a mortal, Coronis. His mother had an affair and, as a consequence, Apollo got very angry and had her murdered. As she was lying on her funeral pyre, Apollo snatched the unborn Asclepius from her womb and gave it to a centaur, a creature who is half human and half horse. The centaur raised the child and taught him healing incantations, and how to use herbs and potions. Asclepius grew up to be a great physician. He supposedly raised someone from the dead and, as a consequence, the king of the Olympian Gods, Zeus, had him killed. In death Asclepius was deified. In late classical times, the devotees of Asclepius were the most resistant opponents of Christianity. He was the last pagan god to fall to the Christian world. He was so difficult to destroy, we are told, because people continued to be healed in his temples.

After her visions of books, Dr. Schucman had another, in which she found herself walking into a seaside cave where she found a scroll. She opened the scroll and read the words written there, in the middle of the parchment: "God is." Tiny words began to appear in columns down the side of the scroll, and she heard a voice saying, "If you roll it out, you will know the future and the past." Dr. Schucman unrolled the scroll all the way, hesitated a moment, then decided she had no interest in reading backward or forward in time. She rolled the parchment up again.

The voice said to her, "You made it this time. Thank you."

A couple of weeks later, after more visions, Dr. Schucman heard the same voice speaking to her again. It said, "This is a course in miracles. Please take notes." The voice apparently kept repeating this.

Dr. Schucman called up her colleague, Bill Thetford, on the phone and asked him, "What do I do? I'm hearing this voice."

Dr. Thetford said, "Well, why don't you take notes? Why don't you see what it's all about?"

That evening the transcription of *A Course in Miracles* began. Almost every morning for the next seven years, Dr. Schucman came to her office at 7:30 and transcribed her invisible teacher's words. They were written out in shorthand and then typed up on a typewriter.

If you read *A Course in Miracles* and the literature that has grown up round it, you might think the author was Jesus of Nazareth. He does call himself Jesus. Course in Miracles devotees, however, are cautious about identifying this figure with the historical son of God of the New Testament. The Jesus of the Course in Miracles explains that his biblical counterpart was misunderstood and misquoted. If either character is fictional, he implies, it is more likely to be the one whose story was written down two thousand years ago.

Chapter Two
Teachings of the Course

Dr. William Thetford spent the next twenty years disseminating the teachings of the Course in Miracles, and after he retired, moved to La Jolla, California, just north of San Diego. At the height of my New Age career, I was involved in study groups in which he was directly involved. I also took a number of other workshops and seminars on the Course in Miracles, and although I was never a Course teacher, I learned its basic principles. Perhaps it is because I spent so much time and effort in studying the Course in Miracles that its radical differences from Church teaching are so clear and disturbing to me.

The first principle to mention is that God lives in heaven, and all of God's children – you, I, his Son — all live there with him, right now. We are asleep, and our bad dream is that we are separated from God. In this dream we collectively create our world, which is fundamentally an illusion. When we wake up we will discover that we have been in Heaven all along, and our true essence is Love. We don't have to die in order to go to Heaven. We just need to wake up.

Each of us is exactly and entirely the way God created us to be: sinless and wholly innocent. The Course is adamant about this. There is no sin. That is just part of the dream, so, of course, Jesus Christ didn't die for our redemption. He died to demonstrate to us that we are not truly flesh. He died to show us that the most barbaric attack one can imagine on a human being is without effect. The whole purpose of the crucifixion was to prove that God is Love and we are like God.

The Course teaches that, since there is no sin, God has no need to forgive. Original sin is a fiction, and we have never fallen from grace. Our guilt and suffering, therefore, have no purpose. These ideas are just part of the earthly nightmare we have created for ourselves.

Forgiveness, however, does have a function in the world of the Course in Miracles, and that's one feature that, I think, has misled some Christians. The Course uses the word "forgiveness" all the time. One way for us to go home to God is for us to forgive our brothers, all the other holy children of God. In this way we overcome the illusion of sin. But it's not the same as Christian forgiveness. Let's say, for example, that someone were to come and slap me across the face. As a Christian, I would forgive them for that action, which was slapping me across the face. In *A Course in Miracles* I would realize: a. I am not a body; b. this event was an illusion; c. therefore, I can readily forgive someone for something that did not happen. By extension it's the same with crime, poverty, homelessness, war — they are ultimately not real. They are our own creations in this dream world we inhabit. Social justice is a waste of time.

A friend of mine, a former Course in Miracles teacher, tells the story of a conversation she had with a student that chilled her to the bone. She was telling him about the experience of a young Catholic nun in Bosnia who had been raped by Serbian soldiers, become pregnant, and was forced to leave her convent. This nun was quoted as saying, "I will love and I will teach my child to love. We will not perpetuate this."

Her Course in Miracles student explained his own point of view: "This nun, on some level, must have created this experience. It wouldn't have happened to her if she hadn't willed that it happen."

This kind of teaching is at the heart of the social apathy one finds among so many New Agers. If you see injustice, there's no need to interfere. The Course teaches that you would actually be standing in the way of someone's spiritual growth if you were to come to their aid.

Although the Course talks about the Holy Spirit, it rejects the idea of the Trinity. The Holy Spirit is simply a name for the communication link between God and his human children. God, you see, since he is pure Love, cannot be tainted with any kind of impurity. The Holy Spirit expresses God's impulse to reach out to humanity and heal their unconscious thought. At the same time, it keeps his deluded sons and daughter at arm's length.

The Course completely denies the existence of Satan. Utterly rejected are the ideas of spiritual warfare, the battle for the soul and the need for salvation. The only evil is our separation from God, which is an illusion we have created. There are no legions of fallen angels, like the Bible teaches, who wreak havoc among human beings on earth and work to win over our souls. You can imagine how pleased the Evil One is with this. As people read this, they fall farther and farther from their faith, from the belief that they need the help of a loving savior. In embracing the Course in Miracles they join forces with those who are against them. In seeking salvation they risk losing their souls.

Chapter Three
The Voice of Temptation

There is much more to be said about the Course in Miracles. Seven years of demonic dictation cannot be summarized in a few pages. Suffice it to say that the Course in Miracles is the Evil One's mockery and mimicry polished to perfection for the New Age. People are looking for deliverance from sin; the Course offers that. People are looking for an explanation for suffering in the world; the Course offers that. People are looking for control over their life, and the manifestation techniques taught by the Course are fulfilled often enough to give it credibility. Among Christians, a twenty-first century, information age interpretation of the Gospel is an inviting idea, and, as in every age, the appeal of miracles is hard to resist.

But I ask you not to be fooled. I think if we were to take the idea of the Evil One as shown to us in the Bible, sowing separation from God and confusion in the world, and update his message for the modern world, it would sound a lot like these aphorisms from the Course in Miracles:

"I have given everything I see all the meaning that it has for me."

"Innocence is wisdom because it is unaware of evil, and evil does not exist."

"Holding no one prisoner to guilt, we become free."

"Jesus became what all of you must be. Is he the Christ? O yes, along with you.... He waits for your acceptance of Him as yourself."

"My mind is part of God. I am very holy."

"My holiness envelops everything I see."

"My holiness blesses the world."

"There is nothing my holiness cannot do."

Part Five

The New Age and the Church

Chapter One
A Destructive Presence

In the process of rediscovering my Catholic faith after a twenty-five-year absence, I was often shocked to see how the Church had fallen prey to New Age influences I thought I was leaving behind. That's one of the reasons for this book: I want to help Christians, especially clergy, recognize how New Age thinking has infiltrated the Church. It's an ultimately destructive presence that needs to be addressed whenever it appears.

For example, much of the miracle merchandise sold in Catholic stores now – angel stones, affirmation books and so forth – are designed to change our way of thinking. They obscure the traditional meanings of Christianity, and especially the meaning of miracles. We don't get a miracle because we sit and rub a stone angel and recite affirmations every day. So don't buy that stuff. Ask bookstore owners to remove it from their shelves. They can be persuaded to do so.

I attended a conference a few years ago at Xavier University in Cincinnati, one of the oldest Catholic universities in the country, a relatively conservative campus one would suppose. On our way to the auditorium, we happened to pass by the window of the student bookstore. I was amazed to see how much it looked like a New Age storefront. The featured title was Anne Rice's *Vampire Chronicles*. In those days, even the *Wall Street Journal* was writing about the possibility of demonic

influence on her writings, although the author has since returned to the Catholic faith. Rice's book was surrounded by a
dozen other occult-related works, including *The Dictionary of
Satan*, some astrology titles, and the most popular books on
the goddess movement. Off to the side a flyer posted on the
window promoted a meditation retreat with a German Catholic priest who was also a Zen master. How can someone be a
Catholic priest and a Zen master at the same time? One of
these traditions had to be distorted beyond recognition, if
not both.

The small group I was with decided to take action. First
we approached the two priests in charge of the conference.
We asked them, "What can you do?"

"You're the laypeople," they responded. "This is something you should be able to handle."

We talked to some of the conference staff, and they introduced us to one of the attendees, an alumna and benefac-
tor of the university. She shared our concern and promised to
raise the issue at the next board of trustees meeting. The next
day this woman joined us as we took pictures of the window
display, then came with us to the university President's office.
We said to him, "Here's what's going on down at the bookstore."

He was very receptive to our concerns, and agreed to
look into the matter. By the time we left Cincinnati three days
later, the books and the flyer were gone. So take action. Just
go in and say, "We're not going to support your store if you're

going to carry this stuff." Write letters. Educate people. We can't accept the presence of evil in our bookstores.

In my own parish, I learned that the Friday night program for divorced, single and separated Catholics was using *A Course in Miracles* as one of their textbooks. This wasn't happening only at St. Francis Church in California. I've had priests from all over the country contact me to inquire about the Course. They not only hear from their parishioners what an interesting book it is, they also see neighboring churches sponsoring seminars using it. "What," they want to know, "is this all about?"

Make no mistake. This book is the dictated pronouncements of a demon, transcribed by a Columbia University psychologist in the 1960s and '70s. It claims to be an actual revision and correction of Sacred Scripture, but is completely incompatible with Christian teaching. *A Course in Miracles* is the definitive document of the cult of Me, Myself and I. Its transcriber spent the last years of her life in the deepest of depressions, and in her final days reached out to a Catholic priest, her former student, for help.

Chapter Two
Retreats from the Faith

Perhaps the most successful means of introducing New Age thinking into the Church has been through Christian retreat centers. It seems like you can pick up just about any diocesan newspaper and find a retreat advertised there that makes one wonder, "Is this Christian?" The same holds even more true for progressive Catholic magazines and newspapers.

A priest who runs a Jesuit retreat center in northern California told me they were hosting a workshop with a former nun who had made a pilgrimage to India and was now presenting the ideas of the Nine Gates Mystery School, an institute teaching "Earth-based" spirituality. The audience for this seminar was made up of chaplains who worked in hospitals. The course focused on "medicine cards." These are tarot cards, divination tools. They are a form of shamanism in which each card represents a specific animal spirit or totem. With the help of these cards, and their attendant totem, the chaplains were taught how to help the sick and dying. I cannot understand how a priest could set aside the sacraments and other instruments of the Faith to consult animal spirits — especially in the presence of the dying.

Here in San Diego, at a Catholic center for spiritual direction, you can take courses in yoga, Buddhist meditation, and even mental telepathy. The materials describing these courses don't even address the issue of how these foreign practices can help us as Christians. The acceptance of New Age influences is so deep that I guess it goes without saying.

I'm aware of a convent in Minnesota, and there are others in California and Massachusetts also, where nuns offer Reiki healing workshops. I was trained as a Master Teacher in Reiki, which means I was authorized to perform initiations as well as teach methods. Reiki is definitely an occult practice. Practitioners do not call on the Holy Spirit; they call on spirit guides by name. It has no place in the Christian world.

A Franciscan retreat house in Kentucky offers a "holistic, directed retreat for the body, mind and spirit." The sisters who run the retreat assist women in creating a sacred space together, and they promise to help direct the divine spirit within through sitting meditation and energy healing sessions. This program has its roots in the goddess workshops that go back to the 1970s. You can find dozens of retreats advertised in New Age magazines that use the exact same language.

In Arizona, a convent retreat center teaches "contemplative prayer" with an instructor who isn't a Catholic priest or brother. He's a Buddhist monk from the Vietnamese tradition. He's going to teach the art of mindfulness meditation, known as "Vipassana," and how to deal with anger using the concepts of non-dualism, non-attachment and no-self. This doesn't sound at all like putting on the mind of Christ, or, as Paul says, "taking every thought captive." [2 Corinthians 10, 5]

Chapter Three
A Christian Response to the New Age

The important questions for us as Christians are, "Why do people turn away from the teachings of their faith? Why do so many leave the Church behind and look to Eastern religions, or to the occult, or to any of these esoteric shortcuts to so-called enlightenment?"

My answer is that it comes from the same temptation that lured man away from God's plan in the Garden of Eden. It comes from pride, from the ambition to be like God, through our own efforts, through knowledge. So what can the Church do to respond to this temptation? It clearly runs deep in all people and has done so since the beginning.

Let me suggest that we respond by educating ourselves and one another. Those who leave the faith, I believe, and those who seek out New Age avenues within the church, are looking, above all it seems to me, for mysticism. Somehow they have missed the beautiful wealth of mysticism within the Christian tradition, so they leave to find it in all the wrong places. The Eastern religions and occult sciences promise them, "We've got mysticism. We can offer you an experience of God. Would you like that?"

And some of these groups do provide powerful spiritual experiences. I know that. The problem, however, is that they lead their followers away from Jesus Christ, as far from the one, true God, in fact, as they possibly can.

So I tell religious education teachers, especially those with confirmation classes, "Teach your students about the saints. Pass on the precious stories of the direct relationship a Christian can have with Jesus, Our Lady and the Holy Spirit."

The tremendous, beautiful mysticism of our faith far outweighs that of any other tradition. Look at the incorruptible saints like Bernadette. They're actually still clipping her hair and nails at her burial place in France. Look at the experience of the desert fathers in the early church, or our holy St. Francis, or St. Teresa of Avila. In our own era Padre Pio appeared at the bedside of the dying as far away as Rome while his flesh remained at home in San Giovanni Rotondo; Blessed Teresa of Calcutta provided food and medicine to thousands, certain that whatever resources she needed God would provide. In virtually every parish there are people who can witness to miraculous events brought about through prayer. In Lourdes, in Medjugorje, in Fatima, and in the homes of those who ask Our Lady to intercede throughout the world, God has shown his love and compassion by acting in their lives.

In I Corinthians, chapter 12, Paul encourages his fellow Christians to "strive eagerly for spiritual gifts." Contemporary New Agers understand this call. What they have missed, however, is that God has built a home for us in which to receive and understand and use these gifts. That home is the Church. The healing, the knowledge, the powers of prophecy that lure people into Gnostic sciences are demonic tricks that mimic the true charisms of the Holy Spirit. People need to know this, and as Christians we have a mission to teach them. And as we educate those who strive for spiritual gifts, we also help them to build up the body of Christ, the place in which each of us truly "lives and moves and has our being."

Blessed Teresa of Calcutta directed a hospice for the sick and dying in the heart of the poorest neighborhood in one of the poorest and largest cities in the world. Thousands of Westerners used to visit her every year in order to volunteer. Many of them were New Agers, attracted by Mother Teresa's fame, stopping along the way as they went to find their Indian gurus. The story goes that Mother Teresa gave them Miraculous Medals, and although she taught us to "preach without preaching," she would ask them as they left to continue their search, "Isn't Jesus enough for you?"

SPIRITUAL WARFARE PRAYER

Heavenly Father, I thank you for sending your son Jesus, who won victory over sin and death for my salvation. I thank you for sending your Holy Spirit, who empowers me, guides me, and leads me to fullness of life.

Lord Jesus Christ, I place myself at the foot of Your cross and ask You to cover me with Your Precious Blood which pours forth from Your Most Sacred Heart and Your Most Holy Wounds. Cleanse me, my Jesus, in the living water that flows from your Heart. I ask You to surround me, Lord Jesus, with Your Holy Light.

Heavenly Father, let the healing waters of my baptism now flow back through the maternal and paternal generations to purify my family line of Satan and sin. I come before You, Father, and ask forgiveness for myself, my relatives, and my ancestors, for any calling upon powers that set themselves up in opposition to You or that do not offer true honor to Jesus Christ. In Jesus' Holy Name, I now reclaim any territory that was handed over to Satan and place it under the Lordship of Jesus Christ.

By the power of Your Holy Spirit, reveal to me, Father, any people I need to forgive and any areas of unconfessed sin. Reveal aspects of my life that are not pleasing to You. Father, ways that have given or could give Satan a foothold in my life. Father, I give to You any unforgiveness; I give to You my sins; and, I give to You all ways that Satan has a hold of my life. Thank You, Father for these revelations. Thank You for Your forgiveness and Your love.

Dear Lord, I have a confession to make. Through ignorance, stupidity, or willfulness, I have sought supernatural experiences apart from you. I ask you to help me as I renounce all these things. Cleanse me in body, mind, soul, and spirit.

In the name of Jesus I renounce all contact with witchcraft, magic, ouija boards, tea leaf, and other occult games. I renounce all kinds of fortune telling, palm reading, tea leaf readings, crystal balls, tarot, and other card laying. I renounce all astrology, birth signs, and horoscopes. I renounce the heresy of reincarnation and all healing groups involved in metaphysics and spiritualism. I renounce all transcendental meditation, yoga, Zen and all eastern cults, and religious idol worship. I renounce all water witching or dowsing, levitation, table tipping, body lifting, psychometry (divination through objects), automatic writing, and handwriting analysis. I renounce all literature I have ever read and studied in any of these fields that promote the New Age and occult, and I vow to destroy such books and any New Age/ occult objects. I renounce astral projection, soul and out- of -body travel and other demonic skills. I renounce in the Name of the Lord Jesus Christ, all psychic heredity that I may have; and I break any demonic hold on my family line back to seven generations on both sides of the family. I do now renounce and forsake every psychic, New Age, and occult contact that I know about and those which I do not know about. I renounce every cult that denies the blood of Jesus Christ and every philosophy which denies the deity of the Lord Jesus.

Lord, reveal to me anything else I need to renounce.

In the name of Jesus I am closing any door which I may have opened to Satan through contact with the New Age and occult.

Help me to live, to love, and to serve you from this day forward. Amen.

About the Author

Raised as a Catholic, Moira Noonan began her apprenticeship in New Age practices and ideas as a college student. For more than twenty years she worked in Religious Science ministry, and as a psychic counselor and therapist. She developed expertise in such areas as Hypnotherapy, Past-Life Regression, Astrology, the Course in Miracles, Reiki, channeling, crystals, goddess spirituality, clairvoyance, and other occult practices. In 1993, after a series of powerful experiences, she returned to the Church, and is now a popular speaker in the Christian community, witnessing and evangelizing, explaining the deeper meaning and influences of the New Age movement. Noonan has also told her story via religious cable and radio stations worldwide. *Ransomed from Darkness* is her first book. She lives in San Diego, California.

Inquiries regarding Ms. Noonan's appearance schedule may be sent to: North Bay Books, P. O. Box 21234, El Sobrante, California 94820. Or faxed to: (510) 758-4659.

Available Now on Tape
From Concept Audio

Concept Audio has produced a boxed set of six cassette tapes featuring talks and interviews with Moira Noonan, as she discusses her experiences in the New Age, shares conversion stories, and offers guidance to churches and individuals affected by New Age practices. Please contact Concept Audio Tapes for more information, or to place your order.

Concept Audio Tapes
Phone: 619-691-0725
Fax: 702-975-0316
On the Web: www.conceptaudiotapes.com